NINJA FOODI®

MULTICOOKER

FOR TWO

Cookbook

Healthy, Easy And Delicious

Ninja Foodi™ Recipes for Two

Barbara Styles

Copyright

No part of this publication may be reproduced, stored in a retrieval system or transmitted in any form or by any means, electronic, mechanical, photocopying, recording, scanning or otherwise, except as permitted under Sections 107 or 108 of the 1976 United States Copyright Act, without the prior written permission of the Publisher. Requests to the Publisher for permission should be addressed to the Permissions Department.

Limit of Liability/Disclaimer of Warranty: The Publisher and the author make no representations or warranties with respect to the accuracy or completeness of the contents of this work and specifically disclaim all warranties, including without limitation warranties of fitness for a particular purpose. No warranty may be created or extended by sales or promotional materials. The advice and strategies contained herein may not be suitable for every situation. This work is sold with the understanding that the publisher is not engaged in rendering medical, legal or other professional advice or services.

If professional assistance is required, the services of a competent professional person should be sought. Neither the Publisher nor the author shall be liable for damages arising here from. The fact that an individual, organization or website is referred to in this work as a citation and/or potential source of further information does not mean that the author or the Publisher endorses the information the individual, organization or website may provide or recommendations they/it may make. Further, readers should be aware that Internet websites listed in this work might have changed or disappeared between when this work was written and when it is read.

The author publishes its books in a variety of electronic and print formats. Some content that appears in print may not be available in electronic books, and vice versa.

TRADEMARKS: **Ninja Foodi® is a registered trademark and the Ninja™ logo is a trademark of Mealthy Products. Inc.** All other trademarks are the property of their respective owners. The author is not associated with any product or vendor mentioned in this book. This book is an independent publication and has not been authorized, sponsored, or otherwise approved by Mealthy Products Inc. All trademarks and brands within this book are for clarifying purposes only and are the owned by the owners themselves, not affiliated with this document.

TABLE OF CONTENTS

Introduction

Ninja Foodi® Multicooker For Two will provide you with delicious cooking solutions every single day. If you don't have a lot of time to spend in the kitchen, worried about cooking a bad meal, or are not well-versed with cooking, these recipes are for you!

Extremely Short Prep Times- Mae sure that you note the prep time mentioned at the head of every single recipe.

Novice Book- Every single step that you need to take to prepare each of the meal in this book is very easily explained to make sure that you are able to understand them even if you do not have a lot of cooking experience.

Only use the ingredients that you already have- You can choose a recipe that suits your taste buds or of those whom you want to please. You can even go ahead and cook recipes that only need the ingredients that you already have. There are many different types of recipes in this book and many of them only differ from others by an ingredient or probably two.

Grandma TIPS- You will also find many useful TIPS throughout this cookbook. These are the tips that one learns after using a Pressure Cooker for a long period of time or by cooking on a regular basis.

Less Cook and More Talk- Pressure cookers have proved time and again that they are a perfect friend of those who are not at home throughout the day or people who don't want to spend long, rigorous hours in the kitchen, but still want to offer delicious meals to the family members.

Time Management- With a Ninja Foodi® Multicooker, you can make a meal one evening, store the lift-out part of the cooker in the refrigerator overnight, and then place it again into the electronic component of the cooker in the morning.

Why should you choose Set and forget Recipes Cookbook?

- Preparations are **super-easy** and the required ingredients are easily available at reasonable costs

- Many of the recipes only need a **few ingredients** and they too are **readily available**

- Everyone can enjoy the meal, including the cook as he/she **won't be spending a lot of time** or effort for cooking

- Fully loaded with recipes

- Many of the **ingredients** are generally **available at home**

- Can easily choose one that suits you best

- **Delicious flavors** with minimum fuss

- No matter how crazy or tiring your day was, you can relax and enjoy delicious meals with the ones you love with minimum efforts

Happy Coooking!!!!!

Apples And Cinnamon Oatmeal

PREP: 5 MINUTES • PRESSURE: 12 MINUTES • TOTAL: 17 MINUTES • PRESSURE LEVEL: HIGH • RELEASE: NATURAL

Ingredients

3 cups water
2 tablespoons packed brown sugar
½ teaspoon ground cinnamon
¼ teaspoon kosher salt
¾ cup steel-cut oats
1 small apple, peeled, cored, and diced
1 teaspoon unsalted butter
1-tablespoon heavy (whipping) cream

Directions

1. **Preparing the Ingredients.** In the Ninja Foodi® Multicooker, stir together the water, brown sugar, cinnamon, and kosher salt, dissolving the salt and sugar. Pour in the oats, add the apple, and stir again.
2. **High pressure for 12 minutes.** Lock the lid in place, cook for 12 minutes. To get 12 minutes cook time, press the "Pressure" button. When the time is up turn the Ninja Foodi® Multicooker off. ("Keep warm" setting, turn off).
3. **Pressure Release.** Use the natural release method. Unlock and open the Ninja Foodi® Multicooker .
4. **Finish the dish**. Stir the oats, and taste; if you like them softer, place the lid on the cooker, but *don't lock* it. Let the oats sit for 5 to 10 minutes more. When they are ready to serve, stir in the butter and heavy cream.
Serve and Enjoy!

PER SERVING: CALORIES: 181; FAT: 4G; SODIUM: 157MG; CARBOHYDRATES: 31G; FIBER: 4G; PROTEIN: 5G

Banana Oatmeal

PREP: 5 MINUTES • PRESSURE: 18 MINUTES • TOTAL: 24 MINUTES • PRESSURE LEVEL: HIGH • RELEASE: NATURAL

Ingredients
½ cup steel-cut oats
½ cup packed light brown sugar
2 ripe bananas, chopped
2 teaspoons vanilla extract
½ teaspoon ground cinnamon
¼ teaspoon salt
¼ cup heavy cream

Directions
1. **Preparing the Ingredients.** Mix the oats, brown sugar, bananas, vanilla, cinnamon, and salt with 2¼ cups water in the Ninja Foodi® Multicooker until the brown sugar dissolves.
2. **High pressure for 18 minutes.** Lock the lid onto the pot and cook at high pressure for 18 minutes. To get 18 minutes cook time, press the "Pressure" button and use the TIME ADJUSTMENT button to adjust the cook time to 18 minutes
3. **Pressure Release.** Turn off the Ninja Foodi® Multicooker or unplug it so it doesn't flip to its keep-warm setting. Allow the pot's pressure to come to normal naturally, 10 to 12 minutes.
   If the pot's pressure hasn't returned to normal within 12 minutes, use the quick-release method to bring it back to normal.
4. **Finish the dish.** Unlock and open the cooker. Stir in the cream and set aside for 1 minute to warm before serving.

Egg and Cheese Breakfast

PREP: 5 MINUTES • PRESSURE: 4 MINUTES • TOTAL: 9 MINUTES • PRESSURE LEVEL: HIGH • RELEASE: QUICK

Ingredients

1 teaspoon-unsalted butter, at room temperature, divided
2 large eggs
¼ teaspoon kosher salt, divided
Freshly ground black pepper
2 tablespoons grated aged Cheddar or Parmesan cheese, divided
1-cup water, for steaming
2 English muffins

Directions

1. **Preparing the Ingredients.** Using ½ teaspoon of butter each, coat the insides of 2 heatproof custard cups or small ramekins. Crack 1 egg into each cup, and carefully pierce the yolks in several places to make sure the yolk cooks through evenly. Sprinkle each with ⅛ teaspoon of kosher salt, some pepper, and 1 tablespoon of Cheddar cheese, covering the eggs. Cover the cups with aluminum foil, crimping it around the sides.
Add water and insert the steamer basket or trivet. Place the cups on the insert.
2. **High pressure for 4 minutes**. Lock the lid in place, and bring the pot to high pressure for 4 minutes. To get 4-minutes cook time, press the "Pressure" button and use the COOK TIME ADJUSTMENT button to adjust the cook time to 4 minutes.
3. **Pressure Release.** After the timer reaches 0, the cooker will automatically enter Keep warm mode. Press the CANCEL button and carefully release the pressure.
4. **Finish the dish.** Toast the English muffins while the eggs cook.
Unlock but *don't remove* the lid for another 30 seconds; this helps ensure that the whites are fully cooked. Using tongs, remove the cups from the cooker and peel off the foil.
Using a small offset spatula or knife, loosen the eggs, then tip each one out onto the bottom half of one of the English muffins.
Top with the other half, and enjoy.

PER SERVING: CALORIES: 241; FAT: 9G; SODIUM: 682MG; CARBOHYDRATES: 26G; FIBER: 2G; PROTEIN: 14G

Soft, Medium, And Hard-Boiled Eggs

PREP: 5 MINUTES • PRESSURE: 3 MINUTES • TOTAL: 8 MINUTES • PRESSURE LEVEL: HIGH • RELEASE: VARIOUS

Ingredients
2 cold, large eggs (straight from the refrigerator)

Directions
Preparing the Ingredients. Set a large metal vegetable steamer in the Ninja Foodi® Multicooker; Add about 2 inches of water to the cooker—not so much that it comes through the holes of the steamer. Set one or more eggs in the steamer.

For soft-boiled eggs—Lock the lid onto the pot.

High pressure for 1 1/2 minutes. Bring the cooker to high pressure by pressing the "Pressure" button. Allow to cook for 1 1/2 minute and press START/STOP.

Pressure Release. Use the quick-release method to bring the pressure in the pot back to normal.

For medium-boiled eggs—Lock the lid onto the pot.

High pressure for 3 minutes. Close the lid and the pressure valve and then cook for 3 minutes. To get 3-minutes cook time, press "Pressure" button and adjust the time.

Pressure Release. Use the quick-release method to bring the pot's pressure back to normal—but do not open the pot. Set the cooker aside, covered, for 1 minute. Use the quick-release method to bring the pot's pressure fully back to normal.

For hard-boiled eggs—Lock the lid onto the pot.

High pressure for 3 minutes. Close the lid and the pressure valve and then cook for 3 minutes. To get 3-minutes cook time, press "Pressure" button and use the TIME ADJUSTMENT button to adjust the cook time to 3 minutes.

Pressure Release. Turn off the machine or unplug it; set aside for 8 minutes. Use the quick-release method to bring the pot fully back to normal pressure.

For all eggs—Unlock and remove the lid. Transfer the eggs to a large bowl. Cut the top off a soft-boiled egg and serve it in an egg cup; peel the other kinds of eggs while still warm.

Quinoa Breakfast Bowl

PREP: 15 MINUTES • PRESSURE: 7 MINUTES • TOTAL: 22 MINUTES • PRESSURE LEVEL: HIGH • RELEASE: NATURAL

Ingredients
1-cup (173 g) quinoa
1 1/2 cups (350 ml) water
3/4 teaspoon kosher salt, divided
1-pint cherry tomatoes (25 to 30 tomatoes)
1-tablespoon (15 ml) extra-virgin olive oil
1/4 teaspoon freshly ground black pepper
2 scallions (white and light green parts), thinly sliced
2 tablespoons (8 g) chopped fresh flat-leaf parsley
1 avocado
2 large eggs, hard-boiled, cooled, and peeled

Directions

1. **Preparing the Ingredients.** Using a fine-mesh strainer, rinse the quinoa, then place into the Ninja Foodi® Multicooker . Add the water and 1/2 teaspoon of the salt.
2. **High pressure for 7 minutes.** Close the lid and Cook for 7 minutes. To get 7-minutes cook time, press the "Pressure" button and use the TIME ADJUSTMENT button to adjust the cook time to 7 minutes.
3. **Pressure Release.** Use the "Natural Release" method for 5 minutes, then vent any remaining steam and open the lid.
Fluff with a fork. Press [Cancel], lock the lid, and let sit for 5 minutes more.
4. **Finish the dish.** Toss the tomatoes with the olive oil, pepper, and the remaining 1/4 teaspoon salt. Close the crisping lid. Select BROIL, and set the time to 3 minutes. Select START/STOP to begin. Broil until the tomatoes begin to burst, about 3 minutes. Toss with the scallions and parsley.
Pit, peel, and dice the avocado. Divide the quinoa among bowls, top with the tomatoes and avocado, and then coarsely grate the eggs on top.
Serve and Enjoy!

"Softboiled" Eggs

PREP: 5 MINUTES • PRESSURE: 3 MINUTES • TOTAL: 8 MINUTES • PRESSURE LEVEL: HIGH • RELEASE: QUICK

Ingredients
2 teaspoons unsalted butter, at room temperature, divided
2 large eggs
¼ teaspoon kosher salt, divided
Freshly ground black pepper
1-cup water, for steaming
2 slices of toast (optional)

Directions
1. **Preparing the Ingredients.** Using ½ teaspoon of butter each, coat the insides of 2 heatproof custard cups or small ramekins. Crack 1 egg into each cup, and sprinkle each with ⅛ teaspoon of kosher salt and some pepper. Divide the remaining 1teaspoon of butter in half, and top each egg with one piece. (You can omit the butter on top of the egg, but it is delicious. Don't skip buttering the dish, though, or the egg won't come out.) Cover the cups with aluminum foil, crimping it down around the sides.
   Add the water and insert the steamer basket or trivet. Carefully transfer the cups to the steamer insert.
2. **High pressure for 3 minutes.** Close the lid and the pressure valve and then cook for 3 minutes. To get 3-minutes cook time, press "Pressure" button and the TIME ADJUSTMENT button to adjust the cook time to 3 minutes.
3. **Pressure release.** Use the quick-release method.
4. **Finish the dish.** Unlock but *don't remove* the lid for another 30 seconds; this will help ensure that the whites are fully cooked. Using tongs, remove the cups from the cooker and peel off the foil. Scoop each egg out onto a slice of toast (if desired).
   Serve and Enjoy!

PER SERVING: CALORIES: 105; FAT: 9G; SODIUM: 388MG; CARBOHYDRATES: 0G; FIBER: 0G; PROTEIN: 3G

Tomato, bacon, and Spinach Omelet

PREP: 8 MINUTES • PRESSURE: 5 MINUTES • TOTAL: 30 MINUTES • PRESSURE LEVEL: HIGH • RELEASE: QUICK

Ingredients

4 eggs
2 tbsp. (30 ml) dairy-free milk
2 tbsp. (30 ml) plus 1 tsp (5 ml) ghee, olive oil, avocado oil or lard, divided
¼ cup (50 g) onion, diced
¼ cup (40 g) tomatoes, seeded and diced
3 slices bacon, cooked and crumbled
¼ cup (10 g) fresh baby spinach, chopped
Optional: ham, mushrooms, dairy-free cheese, sliced jalapeños

Directions

1. **Preparing the Ingredients.** In a bowl whisk together your four eggs and dairy-free milk and set it aside. Warm 1 teaspoon (5 ml) of ghee or preferred cooking fat in the stainless steel bowl of your Ninja Foodi® Multicooker by pressing the Sauté button. Spoon in your diced onion and cook for about 5–8 minutes or until it softens, becomes translucent and begins to brown. Remove the cooked onions and set them aside. If you are including mushrooms in your omelet, you may sauté them at the same time as the onions and remove them accordingly. Cooking time may vary, as the mushrooms will release a lot of moisture while cooking.

   Melt the remaining 2 tablespoons (30 ml) of ghee in the Ninja Foodi® Multicooker ®, and then press the Keep Warm/Cancel button once it's completely melted. Now pour in your egg mixture.
2. **High pressure for 5 minutes**. Secure the lid, close the pressure valve and then cook for 5 minutes. To get 5-minutes cook time, press "Pressure" button and the TIME ADJUSTMENT button to adjust the cook time to 5 minutes.
3. **Pressure Release.** Quick-release the pressure and remove the lid once safe to do so.
4. **Finish the dish.** Carefully remove the cooked omelet from the bowl, using a thin flexible spatula. Transfer it to a plate and fill one half with the sautéed onion, diced tomato, bacon and spinach. Then fold the other half over and serve warm.

Grits with Cranberries Breakfast

PREP: 5 MINUTES • PRESSURE: 10 MINUTES • TOTAL: 15 MINUTES • PRESSURE LEVEL: HIGH • RELEASE: QUICK

Ingredients

¾ cup grits or polenta (not quick cook or instant)
3 cups water
⅛ teaspoon kosher salt
½ cup dried cranberries
1 tablespoon unsalted butter
1 tablespoon heavy (whipping) cream
2 tablespoons honey
½ cup slivered almonds, toasted

Directions

1. **Preparing the Ingredients.** In the Ninja Foodi® Multicooker combine the grits, water, kosher salt, and dried cranberries.
2. **High pressure for 10 minutes.** Lock the lid in place, and bring the cooker to high pressure by pressing the "Pressure" button and cook for 10 minutes.
3. **Pressure Release.** Use the quick-release method.
4. **Finish the dish.** Unlock and remove the lid. Quickly add the butter, heavy cream, and honey, and stir vigorously with a wooden spoon or paddle until smooth and creamy. Spoon into bowls, top with the toasted almonds, and serve.

PER SERVING: CALORIES: 251; FAT: 11G; SODIUM: 62MG; CARBOHYDRATES: 35G; FIBER: 3G; PROTEIN: 5G

Delicious Eggs - Breakfast

PREP: 5 MINUTES • PRESSURE: 5 MINUTES • TOTAL: 10 MINUTES • PRESSURE LEVEL: HIGH • RELEASE: QUICK

Ingredients

4 cold large eggs
2 cups whole or low-fat milk
¼ cup sugar
2 teaspoons vanilla extract
⅛ teaspoon salt
¼ teaspoon grated nutmeg

Directions

1. **Preparing the Ingredients.** Set the Ninja Foodi® Multicooker rack in the Pot; pour in 2 cups water.
   Whisk the eggs in a large bowl until smooth, then whisk in the milk, sugar, vanilla, and salt. Divide the mixture among four 1-cup heat-safe ramekins; sprinkle the nutmeg over the tops. Cover the ramekins with foil and set them on the rack, stacking them as necessary so they fit.
   Lock the lid onto the pot.
2. **High pressure for 12 minutes.** Set the Ninja Foodi® Multicooker to cook at high pressure for 12 minutes. To get 12 minutes cook time, press "Pressure" button and adjust the time.
3. **Pressure Release.** Use the quick-release method.
4. **Finish the dish**. Unlock and open the pot. Transfer the ramekins to a wire rack and uncover.
   Serve warm end Enjoy!

Bacon and Onions Quiche

PREP: 5 MINUTES • PRESSURE: 8 MINUTES • TOTAL: 13 MINUTES • PRESSURE LEVEL: HIGH • RELEASE: QUICK

Ingredients

Butter, at room temperature, for coating
2 bacon slices, diced
¼ cup thinly sliced onion
¼ teaspoon kosher salt, plus additional for seasoning
2 large eggs
2 tablespoons whole milk
2 tablespoons heavy (whipping) cream
Freshly ground black or white pepper
1 cup water, for steaming

Directions

1. **Preparing the Ingredients.** Using a small amount of butter, coat the insides of 2 heatproof custard cups or small ramekins.
Set the Ninja Foodi® Multicooker to "Sauté" add the bacon. Cook for 2 to 3 minutes, stirring occasionally, until the bacon renders most of its fat and is mostly crisp. Add the onion, and sprinkle with a pinch or two of kosher salt. Cook for about 3 minutes, stirring, until the onions just begin to brown. Transfer the bacon and onions to paper towels to drain briefly. Wipe out the inside of the Ninja Foodi® Multicooker. If you prefer, sauté the bacon and onions in a small skillet, and you won't have to clean out the Ninja Foodi® Multicooker.
Into a small bowl, crack the eggs. Add the milk, heavy cream, and ¼ teaspoon of kosher salt, and season with the pepper. Whisk until the mixture is homogeneous; no streaks of egg white should remain. Pour one-quarter of the egg mixture into each cup or ramekin. Sprinkle half of the bacon and onions over each, and evenly divide the remaining egg over the bacon and onions.
Add the water and insert the steamer basket or trivet. Carefully transfer the custard cups to the steamer insert. Place a sheet of aluminum foil over the cups. You don't have to crimp it down; it's just to keep steam from condensing on top of the custard.

2. **High pressure for 7 minutes.** Lock the lid in place, and bring the pot to high pressure. Cook at high pressure for 7 minutes. To get 7 minutes cook time, press "Pressure" button and use the COOK TIME ADJUSTMENT button to adjust the cook time to 7 minutes.

3. **Pressure release.** Use the quick-release method.

4. **Finish the dish.** Unlock and remove the lid. Using tongs, carefully remove the custard cups from the Ninja Foodi® Multicooker. Cool for 1 to 2 minutes before serving. If you want to unmold the quiches, run the tip of a thin knife around the inside edge of the cups. One at a time, place a small plate over the top of the cups, and invert the quiches onto the plate.

Enjoy!

PER SERVING: CALORIES: 144; FAT: 12G; SODIUM: 392MG; CARBOHYDRATES: 3G; FIBER: 0G; PROTEIN: 8G

Main Dishes – Meat

Steaks with Garlic Cream Sauce

PREP: 5 MINUTES • COOKTIME: 20 MINUTES • TOTAL: 25 MINUTES

Ingredients:

Olive oil
2 steaks, room temperature
Salt and pepper, to taste
4 garlic cloves, finely chopped
½ tsp fresh oregano, finely chopped
¼ cup dry white wine
¾ cup heavy cream

Directions

1. **Preparing the Ingredients.** Press the "sauté" button on your Ninja Foodi®
   Multicooker and adjust the temperature to HIGH, drizzle some olive oil into the pot.
   Once the oil is very hot, carefully place the steaks into the pot and cook according to
   your preference (rare, medium, well done), turn the steak and cook the other side.
   Remove the steaks from the pot and leave on a board to rest, and sprinkle the steaks
   with salt and pepper at this stage.
   Don't wash the Pot before you make the sauce, the leftover steak juices will add lovely
   flavor to the sauce.
   Keep the Ninja Foodi® Multicooker on the "Sauté" function.
   Add the garlic, herbs, and wine to the pot, sauté until the wine has reduced and the
   smell of alcohol has disappeared.
2. **Finish the dish**. Add the cream, salt, and pepper to the pot and stir to combine.
   Simmer the sauce for about 5 minutes until thick and creamy.
   Serve the steak with a generous helping of creamy garlic sauce spooned over the top.

Mini Pork Roast

PREP: 15 MINUTES • PRESSURE: 20 MINUTES • TOTAL: 35 MINUTES • PRESSURE LEVEL: HIGH • RELEASE: QUICK

Ingredients:

½ cup (4fl oz) apple juice
1 cup (8fl oz) stock (veggie or chicken)
1 apple, cut into 5 pieces
Small pork loin (approximately 1 lb), sprinkled with salt and pepper
Olive oil

Directions

1. **Preparing the Ingredients.** Pour the apple juice and stock into the Ninja Foodi® Multicooker. Place the apple chunks and pork loin into the pot (it will sit in the liquid).
2. **High pressure for 20 minutes.** Secure the lid onto the pot and press the "Pressure"button, adjust the time to 20 minutes.
3. **Pressure Release**. Once the pot beeps, quick-release the pressure and remove the lid. Place the pork loin onto a board to rest as you heat a skillet or fry pan with a drizzle of oil.
4. **Finish the dish.** Once the fry pan is very hot, place the cooked pork loin into the pan and fry on all sides for a minute or so, or until crispy and golden.
   You can utilize the leftover liquid in the Ninja Foodi® Multicooker by pressing the "SAUTE" button and simmering the liquid until reduced (on LOW heat).
   Serve with your favorite vegetables and a drizzle of reduced liquid.
   Any leftover meat will make an amazing sandwich!

Pulled Pork Burgers

PREP: 10 MINUTES • PRESSURE: 45 MINUTES • TOTAL: 55 MINUTES • PRESSURE LEVEL: HIGH • RELEASE: QUICK
SERVES: 2

Ingredients
½ tsp ground cumin
½ tsp ground coriander
½ tsp paprika
2 tbsp tomato ketchup
1 tsp Worcester sauce (or soy sauce as a substitute)
1 tbsp brown sugar
1 cup (8fl oz) apple juice
Salt and pepper, to taste
1 lb pork shoulder
1 onion, roughly chopped
2 brioche buns
2 tbsp mayonnaise (1tbsp per burger)
2 slices of cheddar cheese (or any other cheese)
1 apple, grated

Directions:
1. **Preparing the ingredients.** Place the onion, cumin, coriander, paprika, ketchup, Worcester or soy sauce, brown sugar, apple juice, salt, and pepper into the Pressure Cooker, stir to combine.
   Place the pork shoulder and onion into the pot.
2. **High pressure for 45 minutes.** Secure the lid onto the pot and press the "Pressure" button, adjust the time to 45 minutes.
3. **Pressure release.** Once the pot beeps, quick-release the pressure and remove the lid.
4. **Air Frying and Finish the dish.** Place the pork onto the Broil & crisp basket, close the Crisping Lid, select AIR CRISP, and set the time to 10 minutes. Select START/STOP to begin until golden and crispy and set aside.
   Return the pot to the pressure cooker and Simmer the leftover liquid in the Pressure Cooker on the SAUTE function until reduced and thick.
   With 2 forks, shred the pork meat into pieces.
   Grill the brioche buns under the grill in the oven, or place them cut-side down on a hot, oiled skillet.
   Spread the buns with mayonnaise, then place a generous pile of pulled pork on top, then a sprinkle of grated apple, then the cheese (you could also grill the cheese onto the bun if you want it to be extra melted).

Drizzle some of the reduced liquid from the Pressure Cooker over onto the burger before serving!

Enjoy!

Lamb Steaks with Feta and Potatoes

PREP: 15 MINUTES • COOK TIME: 15 MINUTES • TOTAL: 30 MINUTES • PRESSURE LEVEL: HIGH • RELEASE: QUICK

Ingredients:

2 medium-large potatoes, skin on, cut into cubes
Salt and pepper, to taste
Olive oil
2 lamb steaks
½ tsp dried mixed herbs
3 garlic cloves, sliced
5 oz feta cheese, crumbled

Directions

1. **Preparing the Ingredients.** Pour 2 cups of water into the Ninja Foodi® Multicooker and place the steaming basket into the pot. Place the potato cubes into the steaming basket and sprinkle with salt.
2. **High pressure for 3 minutes.** Secure the lid onto the pot and press the "Pressure"button, adjust the time to 3 minutes.
3. **Pressure Release.** Once the pot beeps, quick-release the pressure and remove the lid. Take the basket of potatoes out of the pot and set aside, discard any leftover water from the pot.
   Drizzle some olive oil into the Ninja Foodi® Multicooker and press the "SAUTE" button, adjust the temperature to HIGH.
   Sprinkle the lamb with salt, pepper, and herbs, and once the oil is hot, add the steaks to the pot and cook for about 1 minute each side, (or more if you prefer more well-done meat).
   Remove the lamb steaks from the pot and place on a board to rest. Don't wash the pot, just leave it as it is.
   Place the garlic into the pot and adjust the temperature to LOW (the pot should still be on the "SAUTE" function), sauté the garlic for about 30 seconds.
4. **Finish the dish.** Add the steamed potatoes to the pot and stir to coat in oil and garlic, sauté for about 5 minutes until crispy and golden, don't worry if they get a bit mushy, that's part of the charm!
   Before serving, stir the feta cheese into the potatoes.

Pulled Pork Burgers

PREP: 10 MINUTES • PRESSURE: 45 MINUTES • TOTAL: 55 MINUTES • PRESSURE LEVEL: HIGH • RELEASE: QUICK

Ingredients:

½ tsp ground cumin
½ tsp ground coriander
½ tsp paprika
2 tbsp tomato ketchup
1 tsp Worcester sauce (or soy sauce as a substitute)
1 tbsp brown sugar
1 cup (8fl oz) apple juice
Salt and pepper, to taste
1 lb pork shoulder
1 onion, roughly chopped
2 brioche buns
2 tbsp mayonnaise (1tbsp per burger)
2 slices of cheddar cheese (or any other cheese)
1 apple, grated

Directions

1. **Preparing the Ingredients.** Place the onion, cumin, coriander, paprika, ketchup, Worcester or soy sauce, brown sugar, apple juice, salt, and pepper into the Ninja Foodi® Multicooker , stir to combine.
   Place the pork shoulder and onion into the pot.
2. **High pressure for 45 minutes**. Secure the lid onto the pot and press the "Pressure"button, adjust the time to 45 minutes.
3. **Pressure Release.** Once the pot beeps, quick-release the pressure and remove the lid.
4. **Air Frying and Finish the dish**. Lightly grease your air fryer basket and place the pork into the fryer. Close crisping lid. Select AIR CRISP, set temperature to 400°F, and set time to 10 minutes. Select START/STOP to begin.
   Simmer the leftover liquid in the Ninja Foodi® Multicooker on the "Sauté" function until reduced and thick.
   With 2 forks, shred the pork meat into pieces.
   Grill the brioche buns under the grill in the oven, or place them cut-side down on a hot, oiled skillet.

Spread the buns with mayonnaise, then place a generous pile of pulled pork on top, then a sprinkle of grated apple, then the cheese (you could also grill the cheese onto the bun if you want it to be extra melted).

Drizzle some of the reduced liquid from the Ninja Foodi® Multicooker over onto the burger before serving!

Enjoy!

Country Fried Steak

PREP: 5 MINUTES • COOK TIME: 12 MINUTES • TOTAL: 20 MINUTES

SERVES: 2

Ingredients
1 tsp. pepper
2 C. almond milk
2 tbsp. almond flour
6 ounces ground sausage meat
1 tsp. pepper
1 tsp. salt
1 tsp. garlic powder
1 tsp. onion powder
1 C. panko breadcrumbs
1 C. almond flour
3 beaten eggs
6 ounces sirloin steak, pounded till thin

Directions:
1 **Preparing the Ingredients.** Season panko breadcrumbs with spices.
   Dredge steak in flour, then egg, and then seasoned panko mixture.
   Place into air fryer basket.
2 **Air Frying**. Close crisping lid. Select AIR CRISP, set temperature to 370°F, and set time to 12 minutes. Select START/STOP to begin.
   To make sausage gravy, cook sausage and drain off fat, but reserve 2 tablespoons.
   Add flour to sausage and mix until incorporated. Gradually mix in milk over medium to high heat till it becomes thick.
   Season mixture with pepper and cook 3 minutes longer.
   Serve steak topped with gravy and enjoy!

PER SERVING: CALORIES: 395; FAT: 11G; PROTEIN:39G; SUGAR:5G

Air Fryer Roast Beef

PREP: 5 MINUTES • COOK TIME: 45 MINUTES • TOTAL: 50 MINUTES

SERVES: 6

Ingredients
Roast beef
1 tbsp. olive oil
Seasonings of choice

Directions:
1 **Preparing the Ingredients** Ensure your air fryer is preheated to 160 degrees.
   Place roast in bowl and toss with olive oil and desired seasonings.
   Put seasoned roast into air fryer.
2 **Air Frying**. Close crisping lid. Select AIR CRISP, set temperature to 160°F, and set time
   to 30 minutes. Select START/STOP to begin and cook 30 minutes.
   Turn roast when the timer sounds and cook another 15 minutes.

PER SERVING: CALORIES: 267; FAT: 8G; PROTEIN:21G; SUGAR:1G

Air Fryer Burgers

PREP: 5 MINUTES • COOK TIME: 10 MINUTES • TOTAL: 15 MINUTES

Ingredients
½ pound lean ground beef
1 tsp. dried parsley
½ tsp. dried oregano
½ tsp. pepper
½ tsp. salt
½ tsp. onion powder
½ tsp. garlic powder
Few drops of liquid smoke
1 tsp. Worcestershire sauce

Directions:

1 **Preparing the Ingredients.** Ensure your air fryer is preheated to 350 degrees.
Mix all seasonings together till combined.
Place beef in a bowl and add seasonings. Mix well, but do not overmix.
Make 4 patties from the mixture and using your thumb, making an indent in the center of each patty.
Add patties to air fryer basket.

2 **Air Frying**. Close crisping lid. Select AIR CRISP, set temperature to 350°F, and set time to 10 minutes. Select START/STOP to begin, and cook 10 minutes. No need to turn!

PER SERVING: CALORIES: 148; FAT: 5G; PROTEIN:24G; SUGAR:1G

Ground Beef Stew

PREP: 5 MINUTES • PRESSURE: 5 MINUTES • PRESSURE LEVEL: HIGH • RELEASE: QUICK

Ingredients

1 tablespoon olive oil

1½ pounds lean ground beef (about 93% lean)

1 large yellow onion, chopped

1 large sweet potato (about 1 pound), peeled and shredded through the large holes of a box grater

1 teaspoon ground cinnamon

1 teaspoon ground cumin

½ teaspoon dried sage

½ teaspoon dried oregano

½ teaspoon salt

½ teaspoon ground black pepper

2 tablespoons yellow cornmeal

2 tablespoons honey

2½ cups beef broth

Directions

1. **Preparing the Ingredients.** Heat the oil in the Ninja Foodi® Multicooker turned to the "Sauté" function. Crumble in the ground beef; cook, stirring occasionally, until it loses its raw color and browns a bit, about 5 minutes. Add the onion; cook, stirring often, until softened, about 3 minutes.

   Stir in the sweet potato, cinnamon, cumin, sage, oregano, salt, and pepper. Cook for 1 minute, stirring constantly. Stir in the cornmeal and honey; cook for 1 minute, stirring often, to dissolve the cornmeal. Stir in the broth.

2. **High pressure for 5 minutes**. Lock the lid on the Ninja Foodi® Multicooker and then cook for 5 minutes. To get 5-minutes cook time, press "Pressure" button and use the TIME ADJUSTMENT button to adjust the cook time to 5 minutes.

3. **Pressure Release.** Use the quick-release method to drop the pot's pressure to normal. Unlock and open the lid. Stir well and set aside, loosely covered, for 5 minutes before serving.

Roasted Stuffed Peppers

PREP: 5 MINUTES • COOK TIME: 20 MINUTES • TOTAL: 25 MINUTES

Ingredients
2 ounces shredded cheddar cheese
½ tsp. pepper
½ tsp. salt
1 tsp. Worcestershire sauce
½ C. tomato sauce
4 ounces lean ground beef
1 tsp. olive oil
1 minced garlic clove
½ chopped onion
1 green peppers

Directions:

1 **Preparing the Ingredients.** Ensure your air fryer is preheated to 390 degrees. Spray with olive oil.

   Cut stems off bell peppers and remove seeds. Cook in boiling salted water for 3 minutes. Sauté garlic and onion together in a skillet until golden in color.

   Take skillet off the heat. Mix pepper, salt, Worcestershire sauce, ¼ cup of tomato sauce, half of cheese and beef together.

   Divide meat mixture into pepper halves. Top filled peppers with remaining cheese and tomato sauce.

   Place filled peppers in air fryer.

2 **Air Frying**. Close crisping lid. Select AIR CRISP, set temperature to 390°F, and set time to 20 minutes. Select START/STOP to begin ,and bake 15-20 minutes.

PER SERVING: CALORIES: 295; FAT: 8G; PROTEIN:23G; SUGAR:2G

Meatballs With Artichokes

PREP: 5 MINUTES • PRESSURE: 8 MINUTES • PRESSURE LEVEL: HIGH • RELEASE: QUICK

Ingredients

1½ pounds lean ground beef (preferably 93% lean)

½ cup dried orzo

1 medium shallot, peeled and shredded through the large holes of a box grater

1 tablespoon minced fresh dill fronds

2 teaspoons finely grated lemon zest

1 teaspoon minced garlic

1 large egg, at room temperature

2 tablespoons olive oil

One 28-ounce can diced tomatoes (about 3½ cups)

One 9-ounce box frozen artichoke heart quarters, thawed (about 2 cups)

½ cup rosé wine, such as Bandol

¼ cup loosely packed fresh basil leaves, minced

2 tablespoons loosely packed fresh oregano leaves, minced

½ teaspoon salt

½ teaspoon ground black pepper

Directions

1. **Preparing the Ingredients.** Mix the ground beef, orzo, shallot, dill, lemon zest, garlic, and egg in a large bowl until uniform. Form into twelve 2-inch balls.

   Heat the oil in the Ninja Foodi® Multicooker set to the "Sauté" function. Add the meatballs, just as many as will fit without crowding. Brown on all sides, turning occasionally, about 8 minutes. Transfer to a bowl and repeat with the rest of the meatballs.

   Add the tomatoes, artichokes, wine, basil, oregano, salt, and pepper to the cooker; stir well to get any browned bits off the bottom of the pot. Return the meatballs and their juices to the sauce.

2. **High pressure for 8 minutes.** Lock the lid onto the pot. Switch the Ninja Foodi® Multicooker to cook at high pressure for 8 minutes. To get 8-minutes cook time, press "Pressure"button and use the COOK TIME ADJUSTMENT button to adjust the cook time to 8 minutes.

3. **Pressure Release.** Use the quick-release method to drop the pot's pressure back to normal.

4. **Finish the dish.** Unlock and open the pot. Stir gently before scooping the meatballs into serving bowls; ladle the sauce over them.

Easy Osso Bucco

PREP: 10 MINUTES • PRESSURE: 90 MINUTES • TOTAL: 100 MINUTES • PRESSURE LEVEL: HIGH • RELEASE: NATURAL

Ingredients

4 veal or lamb shanks cut to size for the Ninja Foodi® Multicooker
¼ cup flour
½ tsp black pepper
½ tsp salt
½ tsp garlic powder
½ tsp onion powder
1 tsp thyme
1 tsp rosemary
¼ cup olive oil
1 Tbsp. butter
2 medium carrots chopped in large chunks
2 stalks celery cut into large chunks
1 medium to large onion chopped
2 cloves crushed garlic
1 to 2 cups chicken broth (keep in mind of the size of the Ninja Foodi® Multicooker)
2 lbs. red potatoes (washed)
2 Tbsp. butter

Directions

1. **Preparing the Ingredients.** Add the flour and the seasonings to a large bowl. Use a wire whisk to blend everything together.

   Rinse the shanks and dry with a paper towel. Roll each shank in the flour mix and set aside on a plate Preheat a large skillet. Add the oil and bring to almost smoking. Place the shanks in the skillet and brown turning each shank to brown all sides of the shank. Once they are browned, set aside. Add the flour to the remaining oil and make a rue. Once the rue is made add the broth to loosen the rue into a sauce.

   Pour ½ of the sauce on the Ninja Foodi® Multicooker and place each shank into the sauce standing upright. Fill in the gaps with the vegetables. Pour the remaining sauce over the shanks and vegetables.

2. **High pressure for 90 minutes.** Seal the Ninja Foodi® Multicooker and cook for approximately 90 minutes. To get 90-minutes cook time, press "Pressure" button and use the COOK TIME ADJUSTMENT button to adjust the cook time to 90 minutes

3. **Pressure Release.** Turn off the Ninja Foodi® Multicooker or unplug it. Allow its pressure to fall to normal naturally, 15 to 20 minutes.

4. **Finish the dish**. Boil the red potatoes (skin on) until tender. Mash the potatoes adding 2 Tbsp. of butter. Salt and pepper to taste.
   Serve a lamb shank on a bed of potatoes. Add a large spoon of the vegetables. Ladle on some of the sauce from the cooker over the shank, vegetables and potatoes.

   Per Serving Calories: 307.4; Carbohydrates: 5.6g; Fat: 8.7g; Fiber: 9.6g; Protein: 40.3g; Sodium: 840.6mg

Lamb with Mexican Sauce

PREP: 10 MINUTES • PRESSURE: 45 MINUTES • TOTAL: 55 MINUTES • PRESSURE LEVEL: HIGH • RELEASE: NATURAL

Ingredients

2 lamb shoulder
1 Spanish onion
3 garlic cloves, minced
1 19 oz. can Old El Paso Enchilada sauce
2 Tbsp. oil
Salt to taste
Cilantro, chopped without the stems
Corn tortillas (2 per person)
Limes cut into 8ths
Black beans or refried beans
Chipotle style rice

Directions

1. **Preparing the Ingredients.** Marinate lamb overnight in Old El Paso Enchilada sauce (mild, medium or hot).
   Turn on the Ninja Foodi® Multicooker to "sauté" mode.
   Add oil. Put in the onions and cook until soft, add garlic and cook for 1 minute.
   Add the lamb and marinade wait until boil.
2. **High pressure for 45 minutes**. Lock the lid on the Ninja Foodi® Multicooker and then cook for 45 minutes. To get 45-minutes cook time, press "Pressure" button, and use the TIME ADJUSTMENT button to adjust the cook time to 45 minutes.
3. **Pressure release.** Let the pressure to come down naturally for at least 15 minutes, then quick release any pressure left in the pot.
4. **Finish the dish**. Cut the limes, heat the beans, put the hot rice into a serving bowl.
   Set the Lamb aside. Ladle generous amount of sauce over it.
   Heat up 3-4 corn tortillas.
   Put the lamb mixture onto a soft warm corn tortilla, sprinkle on cilantro, then squeeze on lime juice.
   Serve and Enjoy!

Lamb And Eggplant Pasta Casserole

PREP: 10 MINUTES • PRESSURE: 8 MINUTES • TOTAL: 18 MINUTES • PRESSURE LEVEL: HIGH • RELEASE: QUICK

Ingredients

2 tablespoons olive oil

1 medium red onion, chopped

1 tablespoon minced garlic

1½ pounds lean ground lamb

One small eggplant (about ¾ pound), stemmed and diced

¾ cup dry red wine, such as Syrah

2¼ cups chicken broth

½ cup canned tomato paste

1 teaspoon ground cinnamon

½ tablespoon dried oregano

½ teaspoon dried dill

½ teaspoon salt

½ teaspoon ground black pepper

8 ounces dried spiral-shaped pasta, such as rotini

Directions

1. **Preparing the Ingredients.** Heat the oil in the Ninja Foodi® Multicooker turned to the "Sauté" function. Add the onion and cook, stirring often, until softened, about 4 minutes. Add the garlic and cook until aromatic, less than 1 minute.
   Crumble in the ground lamb; cook, stirring occasionally, until it has lost its raw color, about 5 minutes. Add the eggplant and cook for 1 minute, stirring often, to soften a bit. Pour in the red wine and scrape up any browned bits in the pot as it comes to a simmer.
   Stir in the broth, tomato paste, cinnamon, oregano, dill, salt, and pepper until everything is coated in the tomato sauce. Stir in the pasta until coated.

2. **High pressure for 8 minutes.** Lock the lid on the Ninja Foodi® Multicooker and then cook for 8 minutes. To get 8-minutes cook time, press "Pressure" button and use the TIME ADJUSTMENT button to adjust the cook time to 8 minutes.

3. **Pressure Release.** Use the quick-release method.
   Unlock and open the pot. Stir well before serving.

Lamb Curry

PREP: 10 MINUTES • PRESSURE: 40 MINUTES • TOTAL: 50 MINUTES • PRESSURE LEVEL: HIGH • RELEASE: NATURAL

Ingredients

2 small onions
2 garlic cloves, peeled and smashed
1¼ cups plain yogurt
2 teaspoons kosher salt
1 tablespoon freshly squeezed lemon juice
1 tablespoon ground coriander
2 teaspoons ground cumin
1 teaspoon ground allspice
1½ teaspoon freshly ground black pepper
½ teaspoon ground ginger
2 tablespoons cornstarch
½ teaspoon red pepper flakes (optional)
1½ pounds boneless lamb shoulder, cut into 1½-inch cubes
Cooked rice or couscous, for serving
¼ cup chopped fresh mint

Directions

1. **Preparing the Ingredients.** Cut one of the onions into chunks. Place it, along all ingredients except for the lamb, rice, and mint, into a blender jar or food processor. Blend until mostly smooth.

   In a large bowl, pour the yogurt mixture over the lamb cubes. Stir to coat the meat evenly; then cover with plastic wrap or aluminum foil and marinate for 2 hours at room temperature, or in the refrigerator overnight.

   Into the Ninja Foodi® Multicooker , pour the meat and marinade. Slice the remaining onion, and add it to the pot, stirring to combine.

2. **High pressure for 40 minutes**. Lock the lid in place, and bring the pot to high pressure for 40 minutes. To get 40-minutes cook time, press "Pressure"button and use the TIME ADJUSTMENT button to adjust the cook time to 40 minutes.

3. **Pressure Release.** After cooking, use the natural method to release pressure.

4. **Finish the dish**. Unlock and remove the lid. Let the lamb sit for a few minutes to allow the fat to rise, and spoon off and discard the fat. Serve over rice or couscous, and garnish with the mint.

Lamb and Bulgur-Stuffed Acorn Squash

PREP: 15 MINUTES • PRESSURE: 20 MINUTES • TOTAL: 40 MINUTES • PRESSURE LEVEL: HIGH • RELEASE: QUICK

Ingredients

- ½ cup medium or coarse bulgur wheat
- 1 tablespoon olive oil
- ½ cup chopped onion
- 2 tablespoons minced red or green bell pepper
- 1 tablespoon minced garlic
- 2 teaspoons kosher salt, plus additional for seasoning
- 1 pound ground lamb
- 2 teaspoons ground cumin
- ½ teaspoon ground coriander
- ½ cup finely chopped fresh parsley
- ¼ cup minced fresh mint
- 1 large egg white, lightly beaten
- 1 medium acorn squash, halved and seeded
- 1 cup water, for steaming

Directions

1. **Preparing the Ingredients.** In a medium bowl, soak the bulgur wheat in very hot tap water for about 15 minutes, or until softened but still slightly chewy.
   Set the Ninja Foodi® Multicooker to "Sauté," heat the olive oil until it shimmers and flows like water. Add the onion, red bell pepper, and garlic, and sprinkle with a pinch or two of kosher salt. Cook, stirring, for about 2 minutes, or until the vegetables soften.
   Drain the bulgur, and return it to the bowl. Transfer the cooked vegetables to the bowl. Add the lamb, 2 teaspoons of kosher salt, and the cumin, coriander, parsley, mint, and egg white. Stir just to combine; don't overwork the meat, or it may become tough.
   Make sure the two squash halves will sit level and fit in the Ninja Foodi® Multicooker in one layer, trimming if necessary. Evenly divide the meat mixture and stuff it into the squash halves.
   Add the water to the Ninja Foodi® Multicooker, and insert the steamer basket or trivet. Place the squash halves on the steamer insert.
2. **High pressure for 20 minutes.** Lock the lid in place, Cook at high pressure for 20 minutes. To get 20-minutes cook time, press "Pressure" button and adjust the time.
3. **Pressure Release.** Use the quick-release method.
4. **Finish the dish.** Unlock and remove the lid. Using a large slotted spatula, carefully remove the squash halves (they'll be quite soft), and serve.

If you can't find acorn squash, or simply don't like it, you can form the meat mixture into a meatloaf and cook it separately. Use the foil sling as described in the Tomato-Glazed Meatloaf recipe to transfer it in and out of the cooker.

Pork with Apple Juice

PREP: 10 MINUTES • PRESSURE: 20 MINUTES • TOTAL: 40 MINUTES • PRESSURE LEVEL: HIGH • RELEASE: NATURAL

Ingredients

1 tablespoon vegetable oil
4 (6 ounce) pork tenderloins
1 (16 ounce) package sauerkraut, drained
1 cup water
6 fluid ounces apple juice
2 teaspoons fennel seed
12 red new potatoes, halved

Directions

1. **Preparing the Ingredients**. Heat oil in the Ninja Foodi® Multicooker, using Sauté button; brown pork tenderloins in the hot oil, about 5 minutes per side. Distribute sauerkraut around the pieces of pork and pour in water and apple juice; sprinkle with fennel seeds.
2. **High pressure for 15 minutes**. Cover the Ninja Foodi® Multicooker and cook on High Pressure for 15 minutes. To get 15-minutes cook time, press "Pressure" button and adjust the time
3. **Pressure Release**. Use Natural release Method.
4. **High pressure for 5 minutes.** Place potatoes into the cooker, cover the Ninja Foodi® Multicooker and cook on High Pressure for 5 more minutes. To get 5-minutes cook time, press " Pressure"button and use the TIME ADJUSTMENT button to adjust the cook time to 5 minutes.
5. **Pressure Release.** Release pressure, using the Natural release Method.
6. Serve and Enjoy!

Per Serving Calories: 170; Fat: 6g; Sat Fat: 2g; Carb: 2g; Fiber: 0g; Protein: 25g; Sugar: 0g; Sodium: 321 mg; Cholesterol: 70mg

Pork Taquitos

PREP: 10 MINUTES • COOK TIME: 16 MINUTES • TOTAL: 26 MINUTES

Ingredients
1 juiced lime
4 whole wheat tortillas
½ C. shredded mozzarella cheese
10 ounces of cooked and shredded pork tenderloin

Directions:
1 **Preparing the Ingredients.** Ensure your air fryer is preheated to 380 degrees.
   Drizzle pork with lime juice and gently mix.
   Heat up tortillas in the microwave with a dampened paper towel to soften.
   Add about 3 ounces of pork and ¼ cup of shredded cheese to each tortilla. Tightly roll
   them up.
   Spray the air fryer basket with a bit of olive oil.
2 **Air Frying.** Close crisping lid. Select AIR CRISP, set temperature to 380°F, and set time
   to 10 minutes. Select START/STOP to begin. Air fry taquitos 7-10 minutes till tortillas
   turn a slight golden color, making sure to flip halfway through cooking process.

PER SERVING: CALORIES: 309; FAT: 11G; PROTEIN:21G; SUGAR:2G

Keto Parmesan Crusted Pork Chops

PREP: 10 MINUTES • COOK TIME: 15 MINUTES • TOTAL: 25 MINUTES

Ingredients
1 tbsp. grated parmesan cheese

1 C. pork rind crumbs

1 beaten eggs

¼ tsp. chili powder

½ tsp. onion powder

1 tsp. smoked paprika

¼ tsp. pepper

½ tsp. salt

2-4 thick boneless pork chops

Directions:
1 **Preparing the Ingredients.** Ensure your air fryer is preheated to 400 degrees.
   With pepper and salt, season both sides of pork chops.
   In a food processor, pulse pork rinds into crumbs. Mix crumbs with other seasonings.
   Beat eggs and add to another bowl.
   Dip pork chops into eggs then into pork rind crumb mixture.
2 **Air Frying.** Spray down air fryer with olive oil and add pork chops to the basket. Close
   crisping lid. Select AIR CRISP, set temperature to 400°F, and set time to 15 minutes.
   Select START/STOP to begin.

PER SERVING: CALORIES: 422; FAT: 19G; PROTEIN:38G; SUGAR:2G

Chinese Salt and Pepper Pork Chop Stir-fry

PREP: 10 MINUTES • COOK TIME: 15 MINUTES • TOTAL: 25 MINUTES

Ingredients
Pork Chops:
Olive oil
¾ C. almond flour
¼ tsp. pepper
½ tsp. salt
1 egg white
Pork Chops
Stir-fry:
¼ tsp. pepper
1 tsp. sea salt
2 tbsp. olive oil
2 sliced scallions
2 sliced jalapeno peppers

Directions:
1 **Preparing the Ingredients.** Coat the air fryer basket with olive oil.
   Whisk pepper, salt, and egg white together till foamy.
   Cut pork chops into pieces, leaving just a bit on bones. Pat dry.
   Add pieces of pork to egg white mixture, coating well. Let sit for marinade 20 minutes.
   Put marinated chops into a large bowl and add almond flour. Dredge and shake off excess and place into air fryer.
2 **Air Frying.** Close crisping lid. Select AIR CRISP, set temperature to 360°F, and set time to 12 minutes. Select START/STOP to begin. Cook 12 minutes at 360 degrees.
   Turn up the heat to 400 degrees and cook another 6 minutes till pork chops are nice and crisp.
   To make stir-fry, remove jalapeno seeds and chop up. Chop scallions and mix with jalapeno pieces.
   Heat a skillet with olive oil. Stir-fry pepper, salt, scallions, and jalapenos 60 seconds. Then add fried pork pieces to skills and toss with scallion mixture. Stir-fry 1-2 minutes till well coated and hot.

PER SERVING: CALORIES: 294; FAT: 17G; PROTEIN:36G; SUGAR:4G

Easy Pulled Pork Taco Dinner

PREP: 5 MINUTES • PRESSURE: 45 MINUTES • TOTAL: 50 MINUTES • PRESSURE LEVEL: HIGH • RELEASE: NATURAL

Ingredients
2 tablespoons olive oil
4 lbs. boneless pork shoulder, cut in two pieces
2 cups barbecue sauce, divided
Pinch of black pepper
Pinch of Cayenne pepper
½ cup water

Directions
1. **Preparing the Ingredients.** Preheat the Ninja Foodi® Multicooker by selecting Sauté function.
   Brown the pork on both sides with the oil 2-3 minutes per side. Once browned, set aside.
   Mix 1 cup barbecue sauce and ½ cup water into the Ninja Foodi® Multicooker. Stir to combine and add the pork back into the Ninja Foodi® Multicooker and the rest of the seasoning.
2. **High pressure for 45 minutes**. Cook on High Pressure for 45 minutes. To get 45 minutes cook time, press "Pressure" button and use the TIME ADJUSTMENT button to adjust the cook time to 45 minutes.
3. **Pressure Release.** When cooking is complete, select cancel and use Natural Release about 15 minutes.
4. **Finish the dish.** Remove the pork from the Ninja Foodi® Multicooker and shred with two forks.
   Strain the cooking juice through a sieve and set aside ½ cup of the juice.
   Select sauté function, put the shredded pork back into Ninja Foodi® Multicooker \and add the 1 cup barbecue sauce and the ½ cup of cooking juice and bring it back to a simmer and mix well.
   Put the Ninja Foodi® Multicooker on "Sauté," put the shredded pork back into Ninja Foodi® Multicooker and add the 1 cup barbecue sauce and the ½ cup of cooking juice and bring it back to a simmer and mix well.
   Serve on warm taco shells with your favorite toppings or on toasted rolls.
   For the remaining Jus you can save it and turn it into a gravy for your next meal.

Harvest Ham Dinner

PREP: 10 MINUTES • PRESSURE: 12 MINUTES • TOTAL: 22 MINUTES • PRESSURE LEVEL: HIGH • RELEASE: NATURAL

Ingredients

Ham sliced ¾ inch thick or cubed

1 Tbsp. cooking oil

½ cup pineapple juice from can of sliced/cubed/or crushed pineapple – your preference

If not enough juice then add water

3 sweet potatoes – peeled and cubed or sliced (3/8 inch slices)

1 can sliced/cubed/or crushed pineapple

½ cup brown sugar firmly packed

3 whole cloves – or a ½ tsp of ground cloves Frozen perogies- potatoe or potatoe and cheddar

Directions

1. **Preparing the Ingredients.** Heat the oil in the Ninja Foodi® Multicooker on the Sauté function per side.

   Add the cubed or slices of ham (depends on what presentation you like).

2. **High pressure for 5 minutes.** Add the pineapple juice and cook on High Pressure for 5 minutes. To get 5 minutes cook time, press "Pressure" button and use the TIME ADJUSTMENT button to adjust the cook time to 5 minutes.

3. **Pressure Release.** Reduce pressure by natural release Method.

   Then add the slices or cubes of sweet potatoes, the pineapple with remaining juice. Sprinkle with the brown sugar and add the cloves. Arrange the frozen perogies on top.

4. **High pressure for 7 minutes**. Cook on High Pressure for 7 minutes. To get 7 minutes cook time, press "Pressure"button and use the TIME ADJUSTMENT button to adjust the cook time to 7 minutes and release pressure.

5. **Finish the dish**. Remove from cooker and garnish with dollop of sour cream.

Asian Pork

PREP: 5 MINUTES • PRESSURE: 35 MINUTES • TOTAL: 40 MINUTES • PRESSURE LEVEL: HIGH • RELEASE: NATURAL

Ingredients

¼ cup hoisin sauce

2 tablespoons rice vinegar

1 tablespoon minced fresh ginger

2 teaspoons minced garlic

1 teaspoon Asian chili-garlic sauce, plus additional as desired

¾ pound pork shoulder, trimmed of as much visible fat as possible, cut into 2-inch cubes

4 slider buns or soft dinner rolls

Directions

1. **Preparing the Ingredients.** In the Ninja Foodi® Multicooker, stir together the hoisin sauce, rice vinegar, ginger, garlic, and chili-garlic sauce until thoroughly mixed. Add the pork, and toss to coat.
2. **High pressure for 35 minutes.** Lock the lid in place, and bring the pot to high pressure. Cook at high pressure for 35 minutes. To get 35-minutes cook time, press "Pressure" button and adjust the time.
3. **Pressure Release.** Use the natural-release method.
4. **Finish the dish.** Unlock and remove the lid. Pour the pork and sauce through a coarse sieve; set the pork aside to cool. Return the sauce to the cooker, and let it sit for 1 to 2 minutes so any fat rises to the surface. Skim or blot off as much fat as possible and discard.
   Turn the Ninja Foodi® Multicooker to "Sauté," and simmer the sauce for about 5 minutes, or until it's the consistency of a thick tomato sauce.
   While the sauce thickens, shred the pork, discarding any fat or gristle. Add the shredded pork to the sauce, and heat through. Serve on buns or over rice.

PER SERVING: CALORIES: 680; FAT: 31G; SODIUM: 1,188MG; CARBOHYDRATES: 60G; FIBER: 3G; PROTEIN: 38G

Garlic Putter Pork Chops

PREP: 10 MINUTES • COOK TIME: 7 MINUTES • TOTAL: 17 MINUTES

Ingredients
2 tsp. parsley
2 tsp. grated garlic cloves
1 tbsp. coconut oil
1 tbsp. coconut butter
2 pork chops

Directions:
1 **Preparing the Ingredients.** Ensure your air fryer is preheated to 350 degrees.
   Mix butter, coconut oil, and all seasoning together. Then rub seasoning mixture over all sides of pork chops. Place in foil, seal, and chill for 1 hour.
   Remove pork chops from foil and place into air fryer.
2 **Air Frying**. Close crisping lid. Select AIR CRISP, set temperature to 350°F, and set time to 7 minutes. Select START/STOP to begin. Cook 7 minutes on one side and 8 minutes on the other.
   Drizzle with olive oil and serve alongside a green salad.

PER SERVING: CALORIES: 526; FAT: 23G; PROTEIN:41G; SUGAR:4G

Bacon Wrapped Pork Tenderloin

PREP: 5 MINUTES • COOK TIME: 15 MINUTES • TOTAL: 20 MINUTES

Ingredients
Pork:
1 tbsp. Dijon mustard
3 strips of bacon
1 pork tenderloin
Apple Gravy:
½ - 1 tsp. Dijon mustard
1 tbsp. almond flour
2 tbsp. ghee
1 chopped onion
2-3 Granny Smith apples
1 C. vegetable broth

Directions:
1 **Preparing the Ingredients.** Spread Dijon mustard all over tenderloin and wrap meat with strips of bacon.
2 **Air Frying.** Place into air fryer. Close crisping lid. Select AIR CRISP, set temperature to 360°F, and set time to 15 minutes. Select START/STOP to begin and cook 10-15 minutes at 360 degrees. Use a meat thermometer to check for doneness.
   To make sauce, heat ghee in a pan and add shallots. Cook 1-2 minutes.
   Then add apples, cooking 3-5 minutes until softened.
   Add flour and ghee to make a roux. Add broth and mustard, stirring well to combine.
   When sauce starts to bubble, add 1 cup of sautéed apples, cooking till sauce thickens.
   Once pork tenderloin I cook, allow to sit 5-10 minutes to rest before slicing.
   Serve topped with apple gravy. Devour!

PER SERVING: CALORIES: 552; FAT: 25G; PROTEIN:29G; SUGAR:6G

Cajun Pork Steaks

PREP: 5 MINUTES • COOK TIME: 20 MINUTES • TOTAL: 25 MINUTES

Ingredients
2-4 pork steaks
BBQ sauce:
Cajun seasoning
1 tbsp. vinegar
1 tsp. low-sodium soy sauce
½ C. brown sugar
½ C. vegan ketchup

Directions:
1 **Preparing the Ingredients.** Ensure your air fryer is preheated to 290 degrees.
   Sprinkle pork steaks with Cajun seasoning.
   Combine remaining ingredients and brush onto steaks. Add coated steaks to air fryer.
2 **Air Frying**. Close crisping lid. Select AIR CRISP, set temperature to 290°F, and set time
   to 20 minutes. Select START/STOP to begin. Cook 15-20 minutes till just browned.

PER SERVING: CALORIES: 209; FAT: 11G; PROTEIN:28G; SUGAR:2G

Tandoori BBQ Pork Ribs

PREP: 5 MINUTES • PRESSURE: 25 MINUTES • TOTAL: 30 MINUTES • PRESSURE LEVEL: HIGH • RELEASE: NATURAL

Ingredients
2 pounds (1kilo) Pork Short-Ribs (also called Baby Back Ribs)
2 bay leaves
1" (3cm) ginger, roughly chopped
5 garlic cloves
4 tablespoons Tandoori Spice Mix (or your favorite dry rub)
3 cups water, or as needed
1½ teaspoons salt ½ cup BBQ Sauce (your favorite kind)

Directions

1. **Preparing the Ingredients.** Slice rib slabs to fit in the Ninja Foodi® Multicooker and position them in the cooker as flat as possible (this means you'll use the least amount of water- it will pressure cook faster and concentrate the flavors).
   Add bay leaves, ginger, garlic, salt and two tablespoons of the spice mix.
   Pour-in enough water to cover the meat (about 4 cups).
2. **High pressure for 22 minutes.** Close and lock the lid of the Ninja Foodi® Multicooker. Cook for 22 minutes at high pressure. To get 22-minutes cook time, press"Pressure"button and use the COOK TIME SELECTOR button to adjust the cook time to 22 minutes
3. **Pressure Release.** When time is up, open the Ninja Foodi® Multicooker with the Natural release method.
4. **Finish the dish.** Carefully lift the tender ribs out of the Ninja Foodi® Multicooker and lay them on a cutting board. Cover with foil and let them cool down further for another 5 minutes.
   Pat dry and paint on the BBQ Sauce (or spice paste). Make ahead: Stop here and wrap the meat tightly - refrigerate for up to three days. Grill, broil or barbecue for about 5 minutes per side.
   Serve immediately.

Air Fryer Sweet and Sour Pork

PREP: 10 MINUTES • COOK TIME: 12 MINUTES • TOTAL: 22 MINUTES

Ingredients
3 tbsp. olive oil
1/16 tsp. Chinese Five Spice
¼ tsp. pepper
½ tsp. sea salt
1 tsp. pure sesame oil
2 eggs
1 C. almond flour
1 pounds pork, sliced into chunks
 Sweet and Sour Sauce:
¼ tsp. sea salt
½ tsp. garlic powder
1 tbsp. low-sodium soy sauce
½ C. rice vinegar
5 tbsp. tomato paste
1/8 tsp. water
½ C. sweetener of choice

Directions:

1 **Preparing the Ingredients.** To make the dipping sauce, whisk all sauce ingredients together over medium heat, stirring 5 minutes. Simmer uncovered 5 minutes till thickened.
   Meanwhile, combine almond flour, five spice, pepper, and salt.
   In another bowl, mix eggs with sesame oil.
   Dredge pork in flour mixture and then in egg mixture. Shake any excess off before adding to air fryer basket.
2 **Air Frying**. Close crisping lid. Select AIR CRISP, set temperature to 340°F, and set time to 12 minutes. Select START/STOP to begin.
   Serve with sweet and sour dipping sauce!

   PER SERVING: CALORIES: 371; FAT: 17G; PROTEIN:27G; SUGAR:1G

Teriyaki Pork Rolls

PREP: 10 MINUTES • COOK TIME: 8 MINUTES • TOTAL: 20 MINUTES

Ingredients
1 tsp. almond flour
4 tbsp. low-sodium soy sauce
4 tbsp. mirin
4 tbsp. brown sugar
Thumb-sized amount of ginger, chopped
Pork belly slices
Enoki mushrooms

Directions:
1 **Preparing the Ingredients.** Mix brown sugar, mirin, soy sauce, almond flour, and ginger together until brown sugar dissolves.
   Take pork belly slices and wrap around a bundle of mushrooms. Brush each roll with teriyaki sauce. Chill half an hour.
   Preheat your air fryer to 350 degrees and add marinated pork rolls.
2 **Air Frying**. Close crisping lid. Select AIR CRISP, set temperature to 350°F, and set time to 8 minutes. Select START/STOP to begin.

PER SERVING: CALORIES: 412; FAT: 9G; PROTEIN:19G; SUGAR:4G

Pork with Barbecue Sauce

PREP: 5 MINUTES • PRESSURE: 25 MINUTES • TOTAL: 30 MINUTES • PRESSURE LEVEL: HIGH • RELEASE: NATURAL

Ingredients

1 tablespoon yellow mustard
1 tablespoon Dijon mustard
1 tablespoon honey
3 tablespoons ketchup
1½ teaspoons cider vinegar
½ teaspoon Worcestershire sauce
¼ teaspoon kosher salt
½ teaspoon ground cayenne pepper
¾ pound boneless pork shoulder, trimmed of as much visible fat as possible, cut into 2-inch chunks
Buns or lettuce leaves, for serving

Directions

1. **Preparing the Ingredients.** In the Ninja Foodi® Multicooker, stir together the yellow mustard, Dijon mustard, honey, ketchup, cider vinegar, Worcestershire sauce, kosher salt, and cayenne pepper until thoroughly mixed. Add the pork, and toss to coat.
2. **High pressure for 25 minutes.** Lock the lid in place, and bring the pot to high pressure. Cook at high pressure for 25 minutes. To get 25-minutes cook time, press "Pressure"button and use the TIME ADJUSTMENT button to adjust the cook time to 25 minutes
3. **Pressure Release.** Use the natural-release method.
4. **Finish the dish**. Unlock and remove the lid. Pour the pork and sauce through a coarse sieve; set the pork aside to cool. Return the sauce to the cooker, and let it sit for 1 to 2 minutes so any fat rises to the surface. Skim or blot off as much fat as possible and discard.
   Turn the Ninja Foodi® Multicooker to "Sauté." Simmer the sauce for about 5 minutes, or until it's the consistency of a thick tomato sauce.
   While the sauce thickens, shred the pork, discarding any fat or gristle. Add the shredded pork to the sauce, and heat through.
   Serve on buns, or use as a filling for lettuce wraps.

PER SERVING: CALORIES: 307; FAT: 7G; SODIUM: 841MG; CARBOHYDRATES: 13G; FIBER: 1G; PROTEIN: 46G

Pork Tenderloin And Coconut Rice

Ingredients

2 tablespoons peanut oil
1 pound pork tenderloin, cut into 4 pieces
1 small leek, white and pale green parts only, halved lengthwise, washed and thinly sliced
One 4½-ounce can chopped mild green chiles (about ½ cup)
1 teaspoon dried thyme
1 teaspoon ground cumin
½ teaspoon ground coriander
¼ teaspoon salt
¼ teaspoon ground black pepper
One 15-ounce can black beans, drained and rinsed (about 1¾ cups)
1 cup chicken broth
1 cup regular or low-fat canned coconut milk
1 cup white long-grain rice, such as white basmati rice
2 tablespoons packed light brown sugar

Directions

1. **Preparing the Ingredients.** Heat the oil in the Ninja Foodi® Multicooker turned to the "Sauté"function. Add the pork tenderloin pieces; brown on all sides, turning occasionally, about 6 minutes. Transfer to a plate.

   Add the leek and chiles; cook, stirring often, until the leek softens, about 2 minutes. Stir in the thyme, cumin, coriander, salt, and pepper; cook until aromatic, less than half a minute. Stir in the beans, broth, coconut milk, rice, and brown sugar until the brown sugar dissolves.

   Nestle the pieces of pork in the sauce, submerging the meat and rice as much as possible in the liquid; pour any juices from the meat's plate into the cooker.

2. **High pressure for 15 minutes**. Lock the lid on the Ninja Foodi® Multicooker and then cook for 15 minutes. To get 15-minutes cook time, press " Pressure" button and adjust the time.

3. **Pressure release.** Use the quick-release method to bring the pot's pressure back to normal, but do not open the cooker.

   Set the pot aside for 10 minutes to steam the rice.

4. **Finish the dish.** Unlock and open the cooker. Transfer the pork pieces to four serving plates; spoon the rice and beans around them.

   Enjoy!

Pork Tenderloin with Braised Apples

PREP: 5 MINUTES • PRESSURE: 5 MINUTES • TOTAL: 10 MINUTES • PRESSURE LEVEL: HIGH • RELEASE: QUICK

Ingredients.

For The Brine (optional)
½ cup Diamond Crystal kosher salt, or ¼ cup fine table salt
¼ cup granulated sugar
2 cups very hot tap water
2 cups ice water

For The Pork And Apples
1 (1-pound) pork tenderloin, trimmed of silver skin and halved crosswise
Kosher salt, for salting and seasoning
2 tablespoons unsalted butter
1 cup thinly sliced onion
1 medium Granny Smith apple, or other tart apple, peeled and cut into ¼-inch slices
¾ cup apple juice, cider, or hard cider
½ cup low-sodium chicken broth
2 tablespoons heavy (whipping) cream
1 teaspoon Dijon mustard, plus additional as needed

Directions

1. **Preparing the Ingredients.**
   • To make the brine (if using)
   In a large stainless steel or glass bowl, dissolve the salt and sugar in the hot water; then stir in the ice water. Submerge the pork in the brine, and refrigerate for 2 to 3 hours. Drain and pat dry.
   • To make the pork and apples
   If you choose not to brine the pork, sprinkle it liberally with kosher salt.
   Set to "Sauté" heat the butter just until it stops foaming. Add the pork halves, browning on all sides, about 4 minutes total. Transfer to a plate or rack, and set aside.
   Add the onion slices to the cooker, and cook, stirring, for 2 to 3 minutes, or until they just start to brown. Add the apple slices, and cook for 1 minute. Add the apple juice, and scrape the browned bits from the bottom of the pot. Bring to a simmer, and cook for 2 to 3 minutes, or until the juice has reduced by about one-third. Add the chicken broth, and return the pork tenderloin to the cooker, placing the pieces on top of the apples and onions.

2. **High pressure for 45 minutes.** Lock the lid on the Ninja Foodi® Multicooker and then cook for 5 minutes. To get 5-minutes cook time, press "Pressure" button and use the TIME ADJUSTMENT button to adjust the cook time to 45 minutes.
3. **Pressure Release.** Use the quick-release method.
4. **Finish the dish.** Unlock and remove the lid. Transfer the pork to a plate or rack, and tent it with aluminum foil while you finish the sauce.

   Turn the Ninja Foodi® Multicooker to "Sauté," simmer for about 6 minutes, or until the liquid is reduced by about half. Stir in the heavy cream and mustard, and taste, adding kosher salt or more mustard as needed.

   Slice the pork into ¾-inch pieces, and place on a serving platter. Spoon the apples, onions, and sauce over the pork, and serve.

PER SERVING: CALORIES: 321; FAT: 13G; SODIUM: 754MG; CARBOHYDRATES: 21G; FIBER: 2G; PROTEIN: 32G

Hominy, Peppers, And Pork Stew

PREP: 5 MINUTES • PRESSURE: 12 MINUTES • TOTAL: 17 MINUTES • PRESSURE LEVEL: HIGH • RELEASE: QUICK

Ingredients

2 tablespoons olive oil

1 large yellow or white onion, chopped

1 large green bell pepper, stemmed, cored, and cut into ¼-inch-thick strips

1 large red bell pepper, stemmed, cored, and cut into ¼-inch-thick strips

2 teaspoons minced garlic

2 teaspoons minced, seeded fresh jalapeño chile

2 teaspoons dried oregano

2½ cups canned hominy, drained and rinsed

One 14-ounce can diced tomatoes, drained (about 1¾ cups)

1 cup chicken broth

1 pound boneless center-cut pork loin chops, cut into ¼-inch-thick strips

Directions

1. **Preparing the Ingredients.** Heat the oil in a Ninja Foodi® Multicooker, turned to the browning function. Add the onion and both bell peppers; cook, stirring often, until the onion softens, about 4 minutes.

   Add the garlic, jalapeño, and oregano; stir well until aromatic, less than 20 seconds. Add the hominy, tomatoes, broth, and pork; stir over the heat for 1 minute.

2. **High pressure for 12 minutes.** Lock the lid on the Ninja Foodi® Multicooker and then cook for 12 minutes. To get 12-minutes cook time, press "Pressure"button and use the TIME ADJUSTMENT button to adjust the cook time to 12 minutes.

3. **Pressure release.** Use the quick-release method to bring the pot's pressure back to normal.

4. Unlock and open the cooker. Stir well before serving.

Main Dishes – Poultry

Easy Chicken

PREP: 5 MINUTES • PRESSURE: 15 MINUTES • TOTAL: 20 MINUTES • PRESSURE LEVEL: HIGH • RELEASE: QUICK

Ingredients

    1 lb. boneless skinless chicken breasts, frozen
    1/2 cup water
    1/2 cup flavorful liquid of your choice

Directions

1. **Preparing the Ingredients.** In a measuring cup or small bowl, mix together the water and flavorful liquid of your choice.
   Place the frozen chicken in the Ninja Foodi® Multicooker liner, and pour the liquid over the chicken.
2. **High pressure for 15 minutes.** Close the lid, press the "Pressure" button, adjust the cooking time. For standard chicken breasts (~4-6 oz. each), cook for 15 minutes; for extra-large chicken breasts (~1 lb. each), cook for 30 minutes.
3. **Pressure Release.** Use the quick release method.
4. **Finish the dish.** Transfer the chicken breasts to a plate and shred into bite-sized pieces with two forks. While you shred the chicken, you can optionally turn on Ninja Foodi® Multicooker 's 'Sauté' mode to reduce the sauce if it is too thin for your taste.
   Return the shredded chicken to the sauce and toss to coat.
   Serve and Enjoy!

Mexican Chicken Burgers

PREP: 10 MINUTES • COOK TIME: 10 MINUTES • TOTAL: 20 MINUTES

SERVES: 2

Ingredients
1 jalapeno pepper
1 tsp. cayenne pepper
1 tbsp. mustard powder
1 tbsp. oregano
1 tbsp. thyme
3 tbsp. smoked paprika
1 beaten egg
1 small head of cauliflower
2 chicken breasts

Directions:

1   **Preparing the Ingredients.** Ensure your air fryer is preheated to 350 degrees.

Add seasonings to a blender. Slice cauliflower into florets and add to blender.

Pulse till mixture resembles that of breadcrumbs.

Take out ¾ of cauliflower mixture and add to a bowl. Set to the side. In another bowl, beat your egg and set to the side.

Remove skin and bones from chicken breasts and add to blender with remaining cauliflower mixture. Season with pepper and salt.

Take out mixture and form into burger shapes. Roll each patty in cauliflower crumbs, then the egg, and back into crumbs again.

2   **Air Frying.** Place coated patties into the air fryer. Close crisping lid. Select AIR CRISP, set temperature to 350°F, and set time to 10 minutes. Select START/STOP to begin.

Flip over at 10-minute mark. They are done when crispy!

PER SERVING: CALORIES: 234; FAT: 18G; PROTEIN:24G; SUGAR:1G

Crispy Southern Fried Chicken

PREP: 10 MINUTES • COOK TIME: 25 MINUTES • TOTAL: 35 MINUTES
SERVES: 2

Ingredients

1 tsp. cayenne pepper

2 tbsp. mustard powder

2 tbsp. oregano

2 tbsp. thyme

3 tbsp. coconut milk

1 beaten egg

¼ C. cauliflower

¼ C. gluten-free oats

4 chicken drumsticks

Directions:

1 **Preparing the Ingredients.** Ensure air fryer is preheated to 350 degrees.
   Lay out chicken and season with pepper and salt on all sides.
   Add all other ingredients to a blender, blending till a smooth-like breadcrumb mixture
   is created. Place in a bowl and add a beaten egg to another bowl.
   Dip chicken into breadcrumbs, then into egg, and breadcrumbs once more.

2 **Air Frying.** Place coated drumsticks into air fryer. Close crisping lid. Select AIR CRISP,
   set temperature to 350°F, and set time to 20 minutes. Select START/STOP to begin and
   cook 20 minutes. Bump up the temperature to 390 degrees and cook another 5 minutes
   till crispy.

PER SERVING: CALORIES: 504; FAT: 18G; PROTEIN:35G; SUGAR:5G

Chicken Kabobs

PREP: 10 MINUTES • COOK TIME: 20 MINUTES • TOTAL: 35 MINUTES

SERVES: 2

Ingredients
1 diced chicken breast
2 bell peppers
4 mushrooms
Sesame seeds
1/3 C. low-sodium soy sauce
1/3 C. raw honey

Directions:

1 **Preparing the Ingredients.** Chop up chicken into cubes, seasoning with a few sprays of olive oil, pepper, and salt.

   Dice up bell peppers and cut mushrooms in half.

   Mix soy sauce and honey together till well combined. Add sesame seeds and stir.

   Skewer chicken, peppers, and mushrooms onto wooden skewers.

   Ensure air fryer is preheated to 388 degrees. Coat kabobs with honey-soy sauce.

2 **Air Frying.** Place coated kabobs in air fryer basket. Close crisping lid. Select AIR CRISP, set temperature to 388°F, and set time to 20 minutes. Select START/STOP to begin.

PER SERVING: CALORIES: 296; FAT: 13G; PROTEIN:17G; SUGAR:1G

Honey BBQ Wings

PREP: 15 MINUTES • PRESSURE: 10 MINUTES • TOTAL: 25 MINUTES • PRESSURE LEVEL: HIGH • RELEASE: QUICK
SERVES: 2

Ingredients
1 cup of your favorite bbq sauce
1/2 cup brown sugar
2tbsp.s Worcestershire sauce
1 tbsp. fresh minced garlic
1/2 cup water
1/2 cup of honey
1 lbs. chicken wings (frozen or thawed)
Optional: 1/2 teaspoon crushed cayenne pepper to add some heat

Directions:
1. **Preparing the ingredients**. Add all the ingredients to the Ninja Foodi Multicooker®. Set the valve on top to seal.
2. **High pressure for 12 minutes**. Set pressure on high for 12 minutes or thawed chicken wings: set pressure on high for 10 minutes. To get 12-minutes cook time, press "Pressure" button and adjust the time.
3. **Pressure release**. Use the Quick-release Method. Carefully remove the lid and place the cooked chicken wings on a Cook & Crisp Basket.
4. **Air Frying and Finish the dish.** Baste them with some more BBQ sauce. Close the Crisping Lid, Select BROIL, and set the time to 5 minutes. Select START/STOP to begin. Broil them for 5 minutes to allow the BBQ to caramelize.
   Turn the wings over, baste and then broil for another 2 minutes.
   Serve and Enjoy!

Chicken BBQ

PREP: 5 MINUTES • PRESSURE: 10 MINUTES • TOTAL: 30 MINUTES • PRESSURE LEVEL: HIGH • RELEASE: NATURAL
SERVES: 2

Ingredients
2-3 pound chicken thighs, bone-in or boneless, skinless, fat trimmed off
2 garlic cloves, chopped
1/8 tsp pepper, or more to taste
¼ tsp salt, or more to taste
½ cup PLUS 1½ tbsp water, divided
½ cup barbecue sauce (use your favorite)
1 tbsp olive oil
1 onion, medium-sized, chopped
1½ tbsp cornstarch

Directions:
1. **Preparing the ingredients.** Press the SAUTÉ" key of the Ninja Foodi Multicooker™.
   Add the oil and heat.
   Add the garlic and onion and sauté for about 1 to 2 minutes or until soft.
   Stir in the 1/2 cup of water and barbecue sauce.
   With the meaty side faced up, add the chicken in the pot. Press the CANCEL key to stop
   the "Sauté" function. Cover and lock the lid.
2. **High pressure for 10 minutes**. Press the "Pressure" key, set the pressure to HIGH, and
   set the timer for 10 minutes.
3. **Pressure Release.** When the Ninja Foodi Multicooker™ timer beeps let the pressure
   release naturally. Turn the steam valve to release remaining pressure.
4. **Air Frying and Finish the dish.** Unlock and carefully open the lid. Transfer the chicken
   into the Cook & Crisp Basket. Generously season both sides with salt and pepper.
   Arrange the chicken with the meaty side faced down. Set aside.
   Press the "SAUTÉ" key of the Ninja Foodi Multicooker™. Bring the cooking liquid in pot
   to a boil. In a small-sized bowl, combine the cornstarch with 1 ½ tablespoon of water
   until smooth.
   When the cooking liquid is boiling, add about ½ of the cornstarch mix into the pot; stir
   until the sauce is thick.
   Add more cornstarch mix, if needed. Simmer the sauce until thick. Taste the sauce and,
   if needed, season with salt and pepper to taste. Turn off the Ninja Foodi Multicooker™.
   Brush the top of the chicken with the sauce.

Close the Crisping Lid, Select BROIL, and set the time to 3 minutes. Select START/STOP to begin and broil for about 2-3 minutes or until the chicken is glazed.
Flip the chicken, and brush the other side with the sauce.

Honey-Chipotle Chicken Wings

PREP: 5 MINUTES • PRESSURE: 10 MINUTES • TOTAL: 15 MINUTES • PRESSURE LEVEL: HIGH • RELEASE: QUICK

SERVES: 2

Ingredients

1 cup water, for steaming

3 tablespoons Mexican hot sauce (such as Valentina brand)

2 tablespoons honey

1 teaspoon minced canned chipotle in adobo sauce

Directions:

1. **Preparing the ingredients.** If using whole wings, cut off the tips and discard. Cut the wings at the joint into two pieces each, the "drumette" and the "flat."
   Add the water and insert the steamer basket or trivet. Place the wings on the steamer insert.

2. **High pressure for 10 minutes**. Close the lid and the pressure valve and then cook for 10 minutes. To get 10-minutes cook time, press "Pressure" button and adjust the time.

3. **Pressure Release.** Use the quick-release method.

4. **Air Frying and Finish the dish.** While the wings are cooking, make the sauce. In a large bowl, whisk together the hot sauce, honey, and minced chipotle.
   Unlock and remove the lid. Using tongs, carefully transfer the wing segments to the bowl with the sauce. Toss gently to coat. Transfer the wing segments to the Cook & Crisp Basket. Close the Crisping Lid, Select BROIL, and set the time to 5 minutes. Select START/STOP to begin. Broil them for 5 minutes or until the wings start to brown, and serve.

PER SERVING: CALORIES: 434; FAT: 27G; SODIUM: 1,152MG; CARBOHYDRATES: 19G; FIBER: 1G; PROTEIN: 31G

Garlic-Ginger Drumsticks

PREP: 10 MINUTES • PRESSURE: 15 MINUTES • TOTAL: 30 MINUTES • PRESSURE LEVEL: HIGH • RELEASE: NATURAL

SERVES: 2

Ingredients
2-4 chicken drumsticks, skin on
For the sauce:
2 tbsp rice wine vinegar
2 tbsp honey
2 tbsp brown sugar
2 cloves garlic, minced
¼ cup water
½ onion, chopped
½ cup soy sauce
1 tsp fresh ginger, minced

Directions:

1. **Preparing the ingredients.** In a bowl, mix all of the sauce ingredients until well combined. Pour the sauce in the Ninja Foodi Multicooker™.
   Add the chicken in the pot and push them down to submerge them in the sauce – they do not have to be covered completely with sauce. Cover and lock the lid.
2. **High pressure for 15 minutes.** Press the "Pressure" key, set the pressure to HIGH, and set the timer for 15 minutes.
3. **Pressure Release.** When the Ninja Foodi Multicooker™ timer beeps, let the pressure release naturally for 15 minutes. Turn the steam valve to release remaining pressure. Unlock and carefully open the lid.
4. **Air Frying and Finish the dish.** Press the "SAUTÉ" key and boil until the sauce is reduced. Close the Crisping Lid, Select BROIL, and set the time to 3 minutes. Select START/STOP to begin. Broil each side of the chicken for 3 minutes. .
   Remove the chicken from the pot and put on a serving platter.
   Pour the sauce over the chicken. Serve and enjoy!

Melted Mozzarella Marinara Chicken

PREP: 10 MINUTES • PRESSURE: 5 MINUTES • TOTAL: 30 MINUTES • PRESSURE LEVEL: HIGH • RELEASE: QUICK

SERVES: 2

Ingredients
 2 large chicken breasts, boneless, skinless
1 can (14 ounces) crushed tomatoes in puree
1 cup low-fat Mozzarella, grated
1 cup water
1 tbsp olive oil
1 tsp dried basil
¼ tsp red pepper flakes
¼ tsp salt
2 cloves garlic, crushed or pressed

Directions:
1. **Preparing the ingredients.** Season the chicken breast with salt and pepper.
   Add the oil into the Ninja Foodi Multicooker™, press the "SAUTÉ" key, and heat the oil. Cooking in 2 batches, cook the chicken breast until browned. Transfer onto a plate. If needed, add more oil in the pot.
   Add the garlic; sauté for 1 minute. Add the water, tomatoes, red pepper flakes, basil, or salt. Stir until combined.
   Return the chicken into the Ninja Foodi Multicooker™. Cover and lock the lid.
2. **High pressure for 5 minutes.** Press the "Pressure" key, set the pressure to HIGH, and set the timer for 5 minutes.
3. **Pressure Release.** When the Ninja Foodi Multicooker™ timer beeps, turn the steam valve to Venting to quick release the pressure. Unlock and carefully open the lid.
4. **Air Frying and Finish the dish.** Check the chicken to make sure the meat is cooked and the middle is no longer pink.
   Put the chicken in the Broil & Crip Basket.
   Press the "SAUTÉ" key of the Ninja Foodi Multicooker™. Bring the sauce in the pot to a simmer and cook until thick to your preferred consistency.
   Pour the thickened sauce over the chicken. Sprinkle grated mozzarella cheese over the chicken. Close the Crisping Lid, Select BROIL, and set the time to 3 minutes. Select START/STOP to begin and broil until the cheese starts to brown lightly and melted. Watch carefully because the cheese can brown quickly.

Mustard Chicken Tenders

PREP: 5 MINUTES • COOK TIME: 20 MINUTES • TOTAL: 25 MINUTES

SERVES: 2

Ingredients
½ C. coconut flour
1 tbsp. spicy brown mustard
1 beaten eggs
½ pound of chicken tenders

Directions:

1 **Preparing the Ingredients.** Season tenders with pepper and salt.

   Place a thin layer of mustard onto tenders and then dredge in flour and dip in egg.

2 **Air Frying.** Add to air fryer. Close crisping lid. Select AIR CRISP, set temperature to 390°F, and set time to 20 minutes. Select START/STOP to begin.

PER SERVING: CALORIES: 403; FAT: 20G; PROTEIN:22G; SUGAR:4G

Air Fryer Chicken Parmesan

PREP: 5 MINUTES • COOK TIME: 9 MINUTES • TOTAL: 20 MINUTES

SERVES: 2

Ingredients
½ C. keto marinara
3 tbsp. mozzarella cheese
1 tbsp. melted ghee
1 tbsp. grated parmesan cheese
6 tbsp. gluten-free seasoned breadcrumbs
 4-ounce chicken breasts

Directions:

1 **Preparing the Ingredients.** Ensure air fryer is preheated to 360 degrees. Spray the basket with olive oil.

   Mix parmesan cheese and breadcrumbs together. Melt ghee.

   Brush melted ghee onto the chicken and dip into breadcrumb mixture.

   Place coated chicken in the air fryer and top with olive oil.

2 **Air Frying.** Close crisping lid. Select AIR CRISP, set temperature to 360°F, and set time to 6 minutes. Select START/STOP to begin. Cook 2 breasts for 6 minutes and top each breast with a tablespoon of sauce and 1½ tablespoons of mozzarella cheese. Cook another 3 minutes to melt cheese.

   Keep cooked pieces warm as you repeat the process with remaining breasts.

PER SERVING: CALORIES: 251; FAT: 10G; PROTEIN:31G; SUGAR:0G

Honey-Chipotle Chicken Wings

PREP: 5 MINUTES • PRESSURE: 10 MINUTES • TOTAL: 15 MINUTES • PRESSURE LEVEL: HIGH • RELEASE: QUICK

Ingredients

- 6 whole chicken wings, or 12 wing segments
- 1 cup water, for steaming
- 3 tablespoons Mexican hot sauce (such as Valentina brand)
- 2 tablespoons honey
- 1 teaspoon minced canned chipotle in adobo sauce

Directions

1. **Preparing the Ingredients.** If using whole wings, cut off the tips and discard. Cut the wings at the joint into two pieces each, the "drumette" and the "flat."
   Add the water and insert the steamer basket or trivet. Place the wings on the steamer insert.
2. **High pressure for 10 minutes.** Close the lid and the pressure valve and then cook for 10 minutes. To get 10-minutes cook time, press "Pressure" button and adjust the time.
3. **Pressure Release.** Use the quick-release method.
4. **Finish the dish.** While the wings are cooking, make the sauce. In a large bowl, whisk together the hot sauce, honey, and minced chipotle.
   Unlock and remove the lid. Using tongs, carefully transfer the wing segments to the bowl with the sauce. Toss gently to coat.
   Air Frying and Finish the dish. Transfer the wing segments to a baking rack placed over a sheet pan. Close crisping lid. Select BROIL, set temperature to 400°F, and set time to 5 minutes. Select START/STOP to begin, broil until the wings start to brown, and serve.

PER SERVING: CALORIES: 434; FAT: 27G; SODIUM: 1,152MG; CARBOHYDRATES: 19G; FIBER: 1G; PROTEIN: 31G

Cranberry Braised Turkey Wings

PREP: 10 MINUTES • PRESSURE: 20 MINUTES • TOTAL: 35 MINUTES • PRESSURE LEVEL: HIGH • RELEASE: NATURAL

SERVES: 2

Ingredients
2 Tbsp. Butter
2 Tbsp. Oil
2 Turkey wings (1-2 lbs.)
Salt and Pepper, to taste
1 cup Dry Cranberries or "Crasins" (soaked in boiling water for 5 minutes) or 1½ cup Fresh Cranberries or 1 cup of canned cranberries, rinsed
1 med Onion, roughly sliced
1 cup shelled Walnuts
1 cup Freshly Squeezed Orange juice (or prepared juice with no added sugar)
1 bunch Fresh Thyme

Directions:
1. **Preparing the ingredients.** Set the Ninja Foodi Multicooker® to "Sauté", melt the butter and swirl the olive oil.
   Brown the turkey wings on both sides adding salt and pepper to taste. Make sure that the skin side is nicely colored.
   Remove the wings briefly from the Ninja Foodi Multicooker® and add the onion, then on top of that add the wings, cranberries, walnuts, a little bundle of Thyme.
   Pour the orange juice over the turkey.
2. **High pressure for 20 minutes.** Close and lock the Ninja Foodi Multicooker®. Cook for 20 minutes at high pressure. To get 20-minutes cook time, press "Pressure" button and adjust the time.
3. **Pressure release.** Use the Natural method.
4. **Air Frying and Finish the dish.** Remove the thyme bundle and carefully remove the wings to the Broil & Crisp basket. Reduce the cooking liquid to about half.
   Put the basket into the pot, close the Crisping Lid, Select BROIL, and set the time to 5 minutes. Select START/STOP to begin and broil until the wings are sufficiently caramelized.
   Pour the reduced liquid, walnuts, onions and cranberries over the wings and serve.

Per Serving Calories: 240.3; Fat: 4.8g; Saturated Fat: 1.9g; Carbohydrates: 18.8g; Sodium: 746.8mg; Fiber: 2.5g; Protien: 20.6g; Cholesterol: 32.9mg

Lemon Garlic Chicken

PREP: 15 MINUTES • PRESSURE: 15 MINUTES • TOTAL: 30 MINUTES • PRESSURE LEVEL: LOW • RELEASE: QUICK

Ingredients
1-2 pounds chicken breasts or thighs
1 teaspoon sea salt
1 onion, diced
1 tablespoon avocado oil, lard, or ghee
5 garlic cloves, minced
1/2 cup organic chicken broth or homemade
1 teaspoon dried parsley
1/4 teaspoon paprika
1/4 cup white cooking wine
1 large lemon juiced (or more to taste)
3-4 teaspoons (or more) arrowroot flour

Directions

1. **Preparing the Ingredients.** Set the Ninja Foodi® Multicooker to the "Sauté" function.
   Add the diced onion and cooking fat.
   Sauté the onions for 5-10 minutes or until softened.
   Add in the remaining ingredients except for the arrowroot flour and secure the lid on your Ninja Foodi® Multicooker .
2. **High pressure for 15 minutes**. Close lid and cook at high pressure for 15 minutes in the Ninja Foodi® Multicooker . To get 15-minutes cook time, press " Pressure"button and adjust the time.
3. **Pressure Release.** Use Quick-release method.
4. **Finish the dish.** At this point you may thicken your sauce by making a slurry. To do this remove about 1/4 cup sauce from the pot, add in the arrowroot flour, and then reintroduce the slurry into the remaining liquid.
5. Stir and serve right away.
   Enjoy!

Chicken with Mushrooms

PREP: 10 MINUTES • PRESSURE: 20 MINUTES • TOTAL: 30 MINUTES • PRESSURE LEVEL: LOW • RELEASE: QUICK

Ingredients

- ½ cup flour (all-purpose)
- ½ tsp salt
- ½ tsp pepper
- 6 boneless skinless chicken (cut into bite-sized chunks)
- 2 tbsp. oil
- 1 onion minced
- 1 (10-ounce) can tomato sauce
- 1 tsp vinegar
- 1 (4-ounce can – I used fresh) sliced mushrooms
- 1 tbsp. sugar
- 1 tsp garlic – minced
- 1 tbsp. dried oregano
- 1 tsp dried basil
- 1 tsp chicken bouillon granules
- 1 cup Romano cheese

Directions

1. **Preparing the Ingredients.** Turn your Ninja Foodi® Multicooker onto the "Sauté" feature and place the chicken in oil until chicken starts to brown.
   Add onion and garlic and cook until they start to become translucent.
   Add remaining ingredients except Romano cheese. Stir to combine ingredients.
2. **High pressure for 10 minutes** Close the Ninja Foodi® Multicooker lid. Cook at high pressure for 10 minutes. To get 10-minutes cook time, press "Pressure" button and adjust the time.
3. **Pressure Release.** After cooking, use "keep warm" mode for 10 minutes. Use Quick release Method.
4. **Finish the dish.** Remove lid and add Romano cheese and stir.
   Add the butter-flour paste-mixture to thicken sauce.
5. Serve and Enjoy!

Per Serving Calories: 310; Total Carbohydrates: 40g; Saturated Fat: 3.8g; Fiber: 9.6g; Protein: 28.5g; Sodium: 494mg

One Pot Pressure Cooker Chicken And Rice

PREP: 10 MINUTES • PRESSURE: 25 MINUTES • TOTAL: 35 MINUTES • PRESSURE LEVEL: HIGH • RELEASE: NATURAL

Ingredients

6 dried shiitake mushrooms, marinated
6 - 8 chicken drumsticks, marinated
2 rice measuring cups (360 ml) Jasmine rice, rinse
1 teaspoon Salt
1½ cup (375 ml) water
1 tablespoon ginger, shredded
Green onions for garnish
Marinade:
1 tablespoon light soy sauce
1 teaspoon dark soy sauce
½ teaspoon sugar
½ teaspoon corn starch
1 teaspoon Shaoxing rice wine
A dash of white pepper powder
1 tablespoon ginger, shredded
1 teaspoon five spice powder

Directions

1. **Preparing the Ingredients.** Place the dried shiitake mushrooms in a small bowl. Rehydrate them with cold water for 20 minutes.

   Chop the drumsticks into 2 pieces. Then, marinate the chicken and mushrooms with the marinade sauce for 20 minutes.

   Rinse rice under cold water by gently scrubbing the rice with your fingertips in a circling motion. Pour out the milky water, and continue to rinse until the water is clear. Then, drain the water.

   Add the rice, 1 teaspoon of salt, and marinated chicken and mushrooms, and 1½ cup of water in the Ninja Foodi® Multicooker.

2. **High pressure for 9 minutes.** Lock the lid on the Ninja Foodi® Multicooker and then cook for 9 minutes. To get 9-minutes cook time, press " Pressure" button and use the TIME ADJUSTMENT button to adjust the cook time to 9 minutes.

3. **Pressure Release.** Let the pressure to come down naturally for at least 15 minutes, then quick release any pressure left in the pot.

4. Serve immediately.

Honey Soy Chicken Wings

PREP: 10 MINUTES • PRESSURE: 20 MINUTES • TOTAL: 30 MINUTES • PRESSURE LEVEL: HIGH • RELEASE: NATURAL

Ingredients

1 ½ pound chicken wings
4 cloves garlic, roughly minced
½ large shallot or 1 small shallot, roughly minced
1 – 2 star anise
1 tablespoon ginger, sliced
1 tablespoon honey
½ cup warm water
1 tablespoon peanut oil
1 ½ tablespoon cornstarch
Chicken Wing Marinade
2 tablespoons light soy sauce
1 tablespoon dark soy sauce
1 tablespoon Shaoxing wine
1 teaspoon sugar
¼ teaspoon salt

Directions

1. **Preparing the Ingredients**. Marinate the chicken wings with the Chicken Wing Marinade for 20 minutes.

   Heat the Ninja Foodi® Multicooker using the "Sauté" function.

   Add 1 tablespoon of peanut oil into the pot. Add the marinated chicken wings into the pot. Then, brown the chicken wings for roughly 30 seconds on each side. Flip a few times as you brown them as the soy sauce and sugar can be burnt easily. Remove and set aside.

   Add the minced shallot, star anise and sliced ginger, then stir for roughly a minute. Add the minced garlic and stir until fragrant (roughly 30 seconds).

   Mix 1 tablespoon of honey with ½ cup of warm water, then add it into the pot and deglaze the bottom of the pot with a wooden spoon.

   Place all the chicken wings with all the meat juice and the leftover chicken wing marinade into the pot.

2. **High pressure for 5 minutes**. Lock the lid on the Ninja Foodi® Multicooker and then cook for 5 minutes. To get 5-minutes cook time, press " Pressure" button and use the TIME ADJUSTMENT button to adjust the cook time to 5 minutes.

3. **Pressure Release.** Let the pressure to come down naturally for at least 10 minutes, then quick release any pressure left in the pot.

4. **Finish the dish.** Open the lid carefully and taste one of the honey soy chicken wings and the honey soy sauce. Season with more salt or honey if desired.

   Remove all the chicken wings from the pot and set aside. Turn the Ninja Foodi® Multicooker to its browning function. Mix 1 ½ tablespoon of cornstarch with 1 tablespoon of cold running tap water. Keep mixing and add it into the honey soy sauce one third at a time until desired thickness.

   Turn off the heat and add the chicken wings back into the pot. Coat well with the honey soy sauce and serve immediately!

Penne with Chicken

PREP: 5 MINUTES • PRESSURE: 5 MINUTES • TOTAL: 10 MINUTES • PRESSURE LEVEL: HIGH • RELEASE: QUICK

Ingredients

1 tablespoon all-purpose flour

1 teaspoon kosher salt, divided

⅛ teaspoon granulated garlic or garlic powder

½ teaspoon dried Italian herbs, divided (or ¼ teaspoon dried oregano and ¼ teaspoon dried basil)

⅛ teaspoon freshly ground black pepper

3 (4-ounce) boneless, skinless chicken thighs

1 tablespoon olive oil

1 cup thinly sliced onion

1 small green bell pepper, seeded and cut into 1-inch chunks (about 1½ cups)

3 garlic cloves, minced or pressed (about 1 tablespoon)

½ cup dry white or red wine

1½ cups Quick Marinara Sauce or plain tomato sauce

2 tablespoons minced sun-dried tomatoes (optional)

1¾ cups water

½ pound penne or similar pasta shape

3 cups arugula or baby spinach

Parmigiano-Reggiano or a similar cheese, for garnish

Directions

1. **Preparing the Ingredients.** In a small bowl or jar with a shaker top, mix together the flour, ½ teaspoon of kosher salt, the granulated garlic, ¼ teaspoon of Italian herbs, and the pepper. Sprinkle the flour mixture over both sides of the chicken thighs, coating as evenly as possible.

   Set Ninja Foodi® Multicooker to "sauté," heat the olive oil until it shimmers and flows like water. Add the chicken thighs, and cook for 5 minutes, or until golden brown. Turn the thighs over, and cook the other side for 5 minutes more, or until that side is also golden brown. Remove the thighs to a rack or cutting board, and cool for 3 minutes. With the Ninja Foodi® Multicooker on "sauté," add the onion, green bell pepper, and garlic. Cook for about 3 minutes, stirring, until the onions just start to brown. Pour in the wine, and scrape the bottom of the pan to release the browned bits, cooking until the wine is almost completely evaporated. Add the Quick Marinara Sauce, the remaining ½ teaspoon of kosher salt, the sun-dried tomatoes (if using), the remaining ¼ teaspoon of Italian herbs, the water, the chicken, and the penne.

2. **High pressure for 5 minutes.** Lock the lid on the Ninja Foodi® Multicooker and then cook for 5 minutes. To get 5-minutes cook time, press " Pressure" button and use the TIME ADJUSTMENT button to adjust the cook time to 5 minutes.
3. **Pressure Release.** Use the quick-release method.
4. **Finish the dish.** Unlock and remove the lid. The penne should be almost done, and the sauce will be a little thin. Add the arugula, and stir. With the Ninja Foodi® Multicooker set to "sauté", cook for 3 to 4 minutes, or until the pasta is done to your liking, the arugula is wilted, and the sauce has thickened. Serve topped with grated Parmigiano-Reggiano.

PER SERVING: CALORIES: 510; FAT: 14G; SODIUM: 1,040MG; CARBOHYDRATES: 63G; FIBER: 6G; PROTEIN: 35G

Easy Turkey Breast

PREP: 10 MINUTES • PRESSURE: 65 MINUTES • TOTAL: 75 MINUTES • PRESSURE LEVEL: HIGH • RELEASE: NATURAL

SERVES 2-4

Ingredients

1 frozen turkey breast with frozen gravy packet
1 whole onion

Directions

1. **Preparing the Ingredients**. Place frozen turkey breast, frozen gravy packet and whole onion in the Ninja Foodi® Multicooker.
2. **High pressure for 30 minutes.** Lock the lid on the Ninja Foodi® Multicooker and then cook for 30 minutes. To get 30-minutes cook time, press "Pressure" button and adjust the time.
3. **Pressure Release.** Use natural-release method.
   Remove lid, turn turkey breast over
4. **High pressure for 30 minutes.** Replace lid on the Ninja Foodi® Multicooker and then cook for 30 minutes. To get 30-minutes cook time, press " Pressure" button.
5. **Pressure Release.** Use natural-release method, again.
6. **Finish the dish.** Remove mesh. Remove turkey and slice. Places slices and turkey gravy into serving dish.
7. Enjoy!

Spicy Turkey Chili

PREP: 10 MINUTES • PRESSURE: 45 MINUTES • TOTAL: 55 MINUTES • PRESSURE LEVEL: HIGH • RELEASE: NATURAL

Ingredients
1 tablespoon olive oil
1 medium yellow onion, diced
2 green bell peppers, seeded and diced
2 fresh cayenne peppers, chopped (seeds included)
4 cloves garlic, chopped
1 teaspoon ground cumin
½ teaspoon dried oregano leaves
1 pound ground turkey
¼ cup your favorite hot sauce
1 (15-ounce) can fire-roasted diced tomatoes
1 (15-ounce) can kidney beans, including their liquid
1 cup grated Monterey Jack cheese
¼ cup chopped cilantro

Directions
1. **Preparing the Ingredients.** Set the Ninja Foodi® Multicooker to its "Sauté" setting and add the oil. Add the onions, peppers, and garlic, and sauté until the onions soften and begin to brown, about 10 minutes.
   Add the cumin and oregano and sauté two more minutes, until aromatic.
   Add the ground turkey, breaking it up with a spoon or spatula. Sauté until opaque and cooked through, about 5 minutes.
   Add the hot sauce, canned tomatoes and kidney beans and stir to combine.
2. **High pressure for 45 minutes**. Lock the lid on the Ninja Foodi® Multicooker and then cook for 45 minutes. To get 45-minutes cook time, press "Pressure"button, and use the TIME ADJUSTMENT button to adjust the cook time to 45 minutes.
3. **Pressure release.** Use natural-release method.
4. **Finish the dish.** Top with grated cheese and cilantro, and serve with rice or cornbread, if desired.
   Enjoy!

Turkey Legs

PREP: 10 MINUTES • PRESSURE: 30 MINUTES • TOTAL: 40 MINUTES • PRESSURE LEVEL: HIGH • RELEASE: NATURAL

Ingredients

2 turkey legs
1 tablespoon olive oil
1 small onion, sliced
3 cloves garlic, roughly minced
1 celery stalk, chopped
2 bay leaves
A pinch of rosemary
A pinch of thyme
A dash of sherry wine
1 cup unsalted homemade chicken stock
1 tablespoon light soy sauce
Kosher salt and ground black pepper to taste

Directions

1. **Preparing the Ingredients.** Season the turkey legs with generous amount of kosher salt and ground black pepper.
   Heat up your Ninja Foodi® Multicooker ®, press "Sauté" button.
   Add 1 tablespoon of olive oil into the pot. Ensure to coat the oil over the whole bottom of the pot. Add the seasoned turkey legs into the pot, then let it brown for roughly 2 - 3 minutes per side. Remove and set aside.
   Add the sliced onion and stir. Add a pinch of kosher salt and ground black pepper to season if you like. Cook the onions for roughly one minute until soften. Add garlic, and then stir for 30 seconds until fragrance.
   Add in chopped celery and cook for roughly one minute.
   Add in a dash of sherry wine, deglaze the bottom of the pot with a wooden spoon. Allow it to cook for a moment for the alcohol to evaporate. Add chicken stock and light soy sauce, then taste the seasoning. Add in more salt and pepper if desired.
2. **High pressure for 20 minutes.** Place the turkey legs into the Ninja Foodi® Multicooker, then close lid. Pressure cook at high pressure for 20 minutes. To get 20-minutes cook time, press "Pressure" button and adjust the time.
3. **Pressure Release**. Use Natural-release method for 10 minutes and then quick-release.

Serve and Enjoy!

Cranberry Braised Turkey Wings

PREP: 10 MINUTES • PRESSURE: 25 MINUTES • TOTAL: 35 MINUTES • PRESSURE LEVEL: HIGH • RELEASE: NATURAL

Ingredients
2 Tbsp. Butter
2 Tbsp. Oil
4 Turkey wings (2-3 lbs.)
Salt and Pepper, to taste
1 cup Dry Cranberries or "Crasins" (soaked in boiling water for 5 minutes) or 1½ cup Fresh Cranberries or 1 cup of canned cranberries, rinsed
1 med Onion, roughly sliced
1 cup shelled Walnuts
1 cup Freshly Squeezed Orange juice (or prepared juice with no added sugar)
1 bunch Fresh Thyme

Directions
1. **Preparing the Ingredients.** Set the Ninja Foodi® Multicooker to "Sauté", melt the butter and swirl the olive oil.
   Brown the turkey wings on both sides adding salt and pepper to taste. Make sure that the skin side is nicely colored.
   Remove the wings briefly from the Ninja Foodi® Multicooker and add the onion, then on top of that add the wings, cranberries, walnuts, a little bundle of Thyme.
   Pour the orange juice over the turkey.
2. **High pressure for 20 minutes.** Close and lock the Ninja Foodi® Multicooker ®. Cook for 20 minutes at high pressure. To get 20-minutes cook time, press "Pressure" button.
3. **Pressure Release.** Use the Natural method.
4. **Finish the dish.** Remove the thyme bundle and carefully remove the wings to a serving dish. Slide the serving dish under the broiler for about 5 minutes or until the wings are sufficiently caramelized.
   In the meantime, reduce the cooking liquid to about half.
   Pour the reduced liquid, walnuts, onions and cranberries over the wings and serve.

Per Serving Calories: 240.3; Fat: 4.8g; Saturated Fat: 1.9g; Carbohydrates: 18.8g; Sodium: 746.8mg; Fiber: 2.5g; Protien: 20.6g; Cholesterol: 32.9mg

Chops, Arborio rice, and Cheese Soup

PREP: 5 MINUTES • PRESSURE: 8 MINUTES • TOTAL: 20 MINUTES • PRESSURE LEVEL: HIGH • RELEASE: QUICK

Ingredients
- 2 pork chops
- 1/2 a cup of Arborio rice
- 1 3/4 cups of water
- 1 can of Campbells cheddar cheese soup
- 1/2 of an onion, chopped
- 1/2 of a cup or corn, or the kernels from 1 ear
- 1/4 of a tomato, chopped
- 2 tablespoons olive oil
- Salt and pepper

Directions
1. **Preparing the Ingredients**. Beging by using the "sauté" setting on the Ninja Foodi® Multicooker to sauté the onions and the pork chops until they are light brown in color. Add all of the rest of the ingredients to the Ninja Foodi® Multicooker, mix it well and lock the lid into place.
2. **High pressure for 8 minutes.** Cook at High pressure for 8 minutes. To get 8-minutes cook time, press "Pressure" button and use the TIME ADJUSTMENT button to adjust the cook time to 8 minutes.
3. **Pressure Release.** After the timer goes off you will let the food rest for 2 minutes before using the quick release option.
4. **Finish the dish**. Remove the lid and let sit until all of the liquid is absorbed before serving. Top with Parmesan cheese.
5. Serve and Enjoy!

Roasted Tomato Soup

PREP: 5 MINUTES • PRESSURE: HIGH • TIME UNDER PRESSURE: 10 MINUTES • RELEASE: QUICK

Ingredients.
3 tablespoons olive oil
½ cup sliced onion
Kosher salt
1 medium garlic clove, sliced or minced
¼ cup dry or medium-dry sherry
1 (14.5-ounce) can fire-roasted tomatoes
1 small roasted red bell pepper, cut into chunks (about ¼ cup)
¾ cup Chicken Stock or low-sodium broth
⅛ teaspoon ground cumin
⅛ teaspoon freshly ground black pepper
1 tablespoon heavy (whipping) cream (optional)

Directions

1. **Preparing the Ingredients.** Set the Ninja Foodi® Multicooker to "sauté", heat the olive oil until it shimmers and flows like water. Add the onions, and sprinkle with a pinch or two of kosher salt. Cook for about 5 minutes, stirring, until the onions just begin to brown. Add the garlic, and cook for 1 to 2 minutes more, or until fragrant.

   Pour in the sherry, and simmer for 1 to 2 minutes, or until the sherry is reduced by half, scraping up any browned bits from the bottom of the pan. Add the tomatoes, roasted red bell pepper, and Chicken Stock to the Ninja Foodi® Multicooker

2. **High pressure for 10 minutes.** Lock the lid on the Ninja Foodi® Multicooker and then cook for 10 minutes. To get 10-minutes cook time, press "Pressure" button and adjust the time.

3. **Pressure release.** Use the quick-release method.

4. **Finish the dish.** For a smooth soup, blend using an immersion or standard blender. Add the cumin and pepper, and adjust the salt, if necessary. If you like a creamier soup, stir in the heavy cream.

   If using a standard blender, be careful. Steam can build up and blow the lid off if the soup is very hot. Hold the lid on with a towel, and blend in batches, if necessary; don't fill the jar more than halfway full.

PER SERVING: CALORIES: 287; FAT: 24G; SODIUM: 641MG; CARBOHYDRATES: 16G; FIBER: 4G; PROTEIN: 4G

Carrot Soup

PREP: 5 MINUTES • PRESSURE: HIGH • TIME UNDER PRESSURE: 10 MINUTES • RELEASE: QUICK

Ingredients

2 teaspoons unsalted butter

⅓ cup coarsely chopped onion

8 ounces carrots, peeled and cut into ½-inch-thick coins

¼ teaspoon kosher salt, plus additional as needed

¼ cup dry sherry

1½ cups Chicken Stock or low-sodium broth

⅛ teaspoon vanilla extract

Pinch ground cayenne pepper

¼ cup fresh or pasteurized carrot juice

3 teaspoons plain, whole-milk yogurt, divided

1 teaspoon minced fresh chives (optional)

Directions

1. **Preparing the Ingredients**. Set the Ninja Foodi® Multicooker to "sauté," heat the butter until it stops foaming and just starts to brown. Add the onion and carrots, and sprinkle with ¼ teaspoon of kosher salt. Cook for 4 to 5 minutes, stirring occasionally, until the onion starts to brown and the carrots begin to soften. Turn the heat to high, and add the sherry. Bring to a boil, and cook for 1 to 2 minutes, or until most of the sherry has evaporated. Add the Chicken Stock.

2. **High pressure for 10 minutes.** Lock the lid in place, and bring the pot to high pressure for 10 minutes. To get 10-minutes cook time, press "Pressure"button and adjust the time.

3. **Pressure Release**. Use the quick-release method.

4. **Finish the dish**. Unlock and remove the lid. Stir in the vanilla and cayenne pepper. Remove from the heat, and cool slightly. Using an immersion or standard blender, purée the soup completely. Stir in the carrot juice. Bring just to a simmer, and season with kosher salt, as needed. Ladle into 2 bowls, drizzle each with 1½ teaspoons of yogurt, sprinkle with the chives (if using), and serve.

PER SERVING: CALORIES: 132; FAT: 5G; SODIUM: 630MG; CARBOHYDRATES: 16G; FIBER: 4G; PROTEIN: 6G

Colombian Chicken Soup

PREP: 5 MINUTES • PRESSURE: HIGH • TIME UNDER PRESSURE: 17 MINUTES • RELEASE: QUICK

Ingredients

1 medium yellow onion, cut in half
2 medium carrots, cut in half crosswise
2 ribs celery, cut in half crosswise
3 bone-in chicken breasts (about 2 pounds, or 907 g)
5 cups (1.2 L) water
1 1/2 teaspoons kosher salt
1 1/2 pounds (680 g) Yukon gold potatoes, cut into 1/2-inch (13 mm) pieces
1 ear corn, cut into 4 pieces
1/4 teaspoon freshly ground black pepper
1 avocado
1/4 cup (60 g) sour cream
1 tablespoon (9 g) capers, rinsed
1 teaspoon dried oregano
8 sprigs fresh cilantro
1 lime, quartered

Directions

1. **Preparing the Ingredients.** To the Ninja Foodi® Multicooker, add the onion, carrots, celery, chicken, water, and salt.
2. **High pressure for 15 minutes.** Lock the lid on the Ninja Foodi® Multicooker and then cook for 15 minutes. To get 15-minutes cook time, press "Pressure" button and adjust the time.
3. **Pressure Release.** Use the "Quick Release" method to vent the steam, then open the lid. Transfer the chicken to a large bowl. When cool enough to handle, shred into pieces, discarding the skin and bones.
   Discard the onion, carrots, and celery. Add the potatoes and corn to the broth.
4. **High pressure for 2 minutes.** Lock the lid on the Ninja Foodi® Multicooker and then cook for 2 minutes. To get 2-minutes cook time, press "Pressure" button.
5. **Pressure Release.** Use the "Quick Release" method to vent the steam, then open the lid.
6. **Finish the dish.** Stir in the chicken and pepper.
   Divide the soup among bowls. Peel, pit, and slice the avocado. Top the soup with the avocado, sour cream, capers, oregano, and cilantro.
   Serve with the lime quarters for squeezing.

Enjoy!

Split Pea *and* Ham Soup

PREP: 5 MINUTES • PRESSURE: HIGH • TIME UNDER PRESSURE: 8 MINUTES • RELEASE: NATURAL

Ingredients
1 tablespoon olive oil
½ cup diced onion
1 garlic clove, minced or pressed
½ pound dried split peas, rinsed
¾ cup diced ham
½ cup diced carrot
1 bay leaf
1 tablespoon minced fresh parsley
¼ teaspoon dried thyme
1 quart water
1 teaspoon kosher salt
1 or 2 dashes Tabasco sauce
Freshly ground black pepper

Directions

1. **Preparing the Ingredients.** Set the Ninja Foodi® Multicooker to "sauté," heat the olive oil until it shimmers and flows like water. Add the onion and garlic. Cook for about 2 minutes, stirring, until the onions soften.
2. Add the split peas, ham, carrot, bay leaf, parsley, thyme, water, and kosher salt to the Ninja Foodi® Multicooker.
3. **High pressure for 8 minutes** .Lock the lid in place, and bring the pot to high pressure.
4. Cook at high pressure for 8 minutes. To get 8-minutes cook time, press "Pressure" button and use the TIME ADJUSTMENT button to adjust the cook time to 8 minutes
5. **Pressure Release.** Use the natural method to release pressure.
6. **Finish the dish**. Unlock and remove the lid. Stir in the Tabasco sauce and pepper. Taste, adjust the seasoning as needed, ladle into 2 bowls, and serve.

PER SERVING: CALORIES: 555; FAT: 13G; SODIUM: 1,284MG; CARBOHYDRATES: 76G; FIBER: 31G; PROTEIN: 37G

Fresh Tomato and Basil Sauce

PREP: 5 MINUTES • PRESSURE: 5 MINUTES • TOTAL: 10 MINUTES • PRESSURE LEVEL: HIGH • RELEASE: NATURAL

Ingredients

1½ pounds ripe tomatoes (4 to 5 tomatoes)
½ teaspoon salt
1 bunch fresh basil
2 tablespoons olive oil
3 garlic cloves, coarsely chopped
¼ cup water
1 tablespoon extra-virgin olive oil

Directions

1. **Preparing the Ingredients.** Halve as many of the tomatoes as will cover the base of your Ninja Foodi® Multicooker (3 to 4). Chop the rest in large pieces and transfer them to a bowl, scraping in their liquid, too. Sprinkle the salt over the chopped tomatoes. Reserve 1 sprig of the basil and snip the leaves off the remaining basil, chop them, and set them aside.
   Heat the Ninja Foodi® Multicooker using the "Sauté" function, add the 2 tablespoons of everyday olive oil, and heat briefly. Arrange the tomato halves, cut side down, in the cooker base and let them fry, without stirring, until caramelized, about 4 minutes. Flip the tomatoes over, sprinkle with the garlic, and pour the chopped tomatoes and their juices into the cooker. Add the water if using. Lay the reserved basil sprig on top.

2. **High pressure for 5 minutes.** Close and lock the lid of the Ninja Foodi® Multicooker. Cook at high pressure for 5 minutes. To get 5-minutes cook time, press "Pressure" button and use the TIME ADJUSTMENT button to adjust the cook time to 5 minutes.

3. **Pressure Release.** When the time is up, open the Ninja Foodi® Multicooker with the Natural Release method

4. **Finish the dish.** Fish out and discard the basil stem. Using a fork, break up the tomato halves and their skins. Return the uncovered cooker base to medium-high heat and cook until the contents have reduced to a sauce consistency, about 5 minutes more. Pour the sauce over pasta, sprinkle with the chopped basil, and swirl on the extra-virgin olive oil. Serve immediately.

Bow Tie Pasta

PREP: 5 MINUTES • PRESSURE: 5 MINUTES • TOTAL: 10 MINUTES • PRESSURE LEVEL: HIGH • RELEASE: QUICK

Ingredients

1 tablespoon olive oil
1 cup thinly sliced onion
3 garlic cloves, minced or pressed (about 1 tablespoon)
½ cup dry sherry or white wine
2¼ cups Mushroom Stock
1 cup water
1 teaspoon kosher salt
½ pound bow tie (farfalle) pasta
3 tablespoons sour cream
1 recipe "Sautéed" Mushrooms
2 tablespoons chopped fresh parsley
2 tablespoons grated Parmigiano-Reggiano or similar cheese

Directions

1. **Preparing the Ingredients.** Turn the Ninja Foodi® Multicooker to "sauté," heat the olive oil until it shimmers and flows like water. Add the onion and garlic, and cook for about 3 minutes, stirring, until the onions just start to brown. Pour in the sherry, and cook for 2 to 3 minutes, scraping the bottom of the pan to release the browned bits, until all the sherry is almost evaporated. Add the Mushroom Stock, water, kosher salt, and pasta.
2. **High pressure for 5 minutes.** Lock the lid in place, and bring the pot to high pressure. Cook at high pressure for 5 minutes. To get 5-minutes cook time, press "Pressure" button and use the TIME ADJUSTMENT button to adjust the cook time to 5 minutes
3. **Pressure Release.** Use the quick-release method.
4. **Finish the dish.** Unlock and remove the lid. The pasta should be almost done with the sauce a little bit thin. Ladle 1 cup of the sauce (with no noodles) into a small bowl. Cool for 1 minute, then stir in the sour cream and set aside. Add the "Sautéed" Mushrooms to the Ninja Foodi® Multicooker. With the Ninja Foodi® Multicooker set to "sauté," cook for 3 to 4 minutes, until the pasta is done to your liking and the sauce has thickened. Stir in the sour cream mixture, parsley, and the grated Parmigiano-Reggiano, and serve.

PER SERVING: CALORIES: 255; FAT: 8G; SODIUM: 424MG; CARBOHYDRATES: 39G; FIBER: 1G; PROTEIN: 10G

Ziti with Three Cheeses And Tomato Sauce

PREP: 5 MINUTES • PRESSURE: 5 MINUTES • TOTAL: 10 MINUTES • PRESSURE LEVEL: HIGH • RELEASE: QUICK

Ingredients

1 cup water
1 cup coarsely chopped onions
½ teaspoon salt
8 ounces ziti or other short pasta that normally cooks in 9 to 13 minutes
One can (28 ounces) peeled plum tomatoes (with liquid)
2 to 4 cloves garlic, peeled, or 1-teaspoon garlic powder
1 to 1½ teaspoons Italian Herb Blend
1 cup ricotta (whole milk or low-fat)
¼ cup grated Parmesan or Romano, plus more for garnish
1 cup (about 6 ounces) shredded or finely chopped mozzarella cheese
Freshly ground pepper

Directions

1. **Preparing the Ingredients.** Combine the water, onions, and salt in a 4-quart or larger cooker.
   Bring to a boil. Stir in the ziti. Pour the tomatoes on top of the ziti, crushing the tomatoes in your hand as you empty the can. Do not stir after adding the tomatoes. Add the garlic.
2. **High pressure for 5 minutes**. Lock the lid in place, and bring the pot to high pressure. Cook at high pressure for 5 minutes. To get 5-minutes cook time, press "Pressure" and use the TIME ADJUSTMENT button to adjust the cook time to 5 minutes
3. **Pressure Release.** Quick-release the pressure under cold running water. Remove the lid, tilting it away from you to allow steam to escape.
4. **Finish the dish.** Stir in the Italian Herb Blend, ricotta, and Parmesan. Separate any ziti that are stuck together and release any that are clinging to the bottom of the cooker. Distribute half of the mozzarella on top. Use a rubber spatula or large spoon to scoop ziti from the bottom and set it on top of the mozzarella. Repeat with remaining mozzarella. Season with salt and pepper to taste.
   Let the dish rest in the cooker for 3 to 5 minutes, giving the mixture time to thicken. If the pasta is not uniformly tender, cover the cooker during this period and cook over very low heat, stirring occasionally, until the pasta is done.
   Serve in pasta bowls with a generous dusting of Parmesan on top of each portion.

Italian-Style Pasta Casserole

PREP: 5 MINUTES • PRESSURE: 8 MINUTES • TOTAL: 13 MINUTES • PRESSURE LEVEL: HIGH • RELEASE: QUICK

Ingredients

2 tablespoons olive oil
1 pound lean ground beef (preferably 93% lean)
1 medium yellow onion, chopped
1 medium green bell pepper, stemmed, cored, and chopped
1 medium yellow bell pepper, stemmed, cored, and chopped
2 teaspoons dried basil
1 teaspoon dried oregano or marjoram
1 teaspoon dried thyme
½ teaspoon fennel seeds
½ teaspoon salt
¼ teaspoon red pepper flakes
¾ cup dry, fruit-forward red wine, such as Zinfandel
One 28-ounce can crushed tomatoes (about 3½ cups)
8 ounces dried ziti

Directions

1. **Preparing the Ingredients.** Heat the oil in the Ninja Foodi® Multicooker turned to the "Sauté"function. Add the ground beef; cook, stirring often, until browned, about 5 minutes. Use a slotted spoon to transfer the beef to a bowl.

   Add the onion and chopped peppers to the pot; cook, stirring often, until the onion softens, about 5 minutes. Stir in the basil, oregano or marjoram, thyme, fennel seeds, salt, and red pepper flakes. Pour in the wine and scrape up any browned bits in the pot as the mixture comes to a simmer. Return the ground beef to the pot along with the crushed tomatoes and pasta. Stir well.

2. **High pressure for 8 minutes**. Lock the lid onto the pot. Switch the Ninja Foodi® Multicooker to cook at high pressure for 8 minutes. To get 8-minutes cook time, press "pressure" button and use the TIME ADJUSTMENT button to adjust the cook time to 8 minutes.

3. **Pressure Release.**Turn off or unplug the Ninja Foodi® Multicooker; set aside for 5 minutes.

   Use the quick-release method.

4. **Finish the dish.** Unlock and open the lid. Stir well before serving.

Wild *and* Brown Rice Pilaf

PREP: 5 MINUTES • PRESSURE: 27 MINUTES • TOTAL: 32 MINUTES • PRESSURE LEVEL: HIGH • RELEASE: COMBINATION

Ingredients

- 1 tablespoon olive oil
- ¾ cup diced onion
- 1 garlic clove, minced
- ⅓ cup wild rice
- ⅔ cup water
- ½ teaspoon kosher salt, divided, plus additional for seasoning
- ½ cup brown rice
- ¾ cup low-sodium vegetable broth
- ¼ cup dry white wine
- 1 bay leaf
- 1 fresh thyme sprig, or ¼ teaspoon dried thyme
- 2 tablespoons chopped fresh parsley

Directions

1. **Preparing the Ingredients.** Set the Ninja Foodi® Multicooker to "sauté". Heat the olive oil until it shimmers and flows like water. Add the onion and garlic, and cook for about 3 minutes, stirring, until the garlic is fragrant and the onions soften and separate. Add the wild rice, water, and ¼ teaspoon of kosher salt, and stir.
2. **High pressure for 15 minutes.** Lock the lid on the Ninja Foodi® Multicooker and then cook for 15 minutes. To get 15-minutes cook time, press "Pressure" button and adjust the time.
3. **Pressure Release.** Use the quick-release method.
   Unlock and remove the lid. Stir in the brown rice, vegetable broth, remaining ¼ teaspoon of kosher salt, white wine, bay leaf, and thyme.
4. **High pressure for 12 minutes.** Lock the lid on the Ninja Foodi® Multicooker and then cook for 12 minutes. To get 12-minutes cook time, press "Pressure" button and use the TIME ADJUSTMENT button to adjust the cook time to 12 minutes.
   When the timer goes off, turn the cooker off. ("Warm" setting, turn off).
5. **Pressure Release.** After cooking, use the natural method to release pressure for 12 minutes, then the quick method to release the remaining pressure.
6. **Finish the dish.** Unlock and remove the lid. Remove the bay leaf and thyme sprig, and stir in the parsley. Taste and adjust the seasoning, as needed. Replace but *do not lock* the lid. Let the rice steam for about 4 minutes, fluff gently with a fork, and serve.

PER SERVING: CALORIES: 195; FAT: 4G; SODIUM: 309MG; CARBOHYDRATES: 32G; FIBER: 2G; PROTEIN: 5G

Spanish Rice

PREP: 5 MINUTES • PRESSURE: 8 MINUTES • TOTAL: 13 MINUTES • PRESSURE LEVEL: HIGH • RELEASE:QUICK

Ingredients

- 1 tablespoon olive oil
- ⅓ cup chopped onion
- 1 large garlic clove, minced
- 1 small jalapeño pepper, seeded and chopped (about 1 tablespoon)
- ½ teaspoon kosher salt, plus additional for seasoning
- ¾ cup long-grain white rice
- ¼ cup plus 2 tablespoons Red Table Salsa
- ¾ cup low-sodium vegetable broth
- 1 tablespoon chopped fresh parsley

Directions

1. **Preparing the Ingredients**. Turn the Ninja Foodi® Multicooker to "sauté," heat the olive oil until it shimmers and flows like water. Add the onion, garlic, and jalapeño, and sprinkle with a pinch or two of kosher salt. Cook for about 3 minutes, stirring, until the vegetables just begin to brown.

   Add the rice, and stir to coat with the olive oil. Add the Red Table Salsa, and cook for 30 seconds, stirring. Add the vegetable broth and ½ teaspoon of kosher salt, and stir to combine.

2. **High pressure for 8 minutes** Lock the lid in place, and bring the pot to high pressure. Cook at high pressure for 8 minutes. To get 8 minutes cook time, press "pressure" button and use the TIME ADJUSTMENT button to adjust the cook time to 8 minutes.

3. **Pressure Release.** Use the quick-release method.

4. **Finish the dish.** Unlock and remove the lid. Gently stir in the parsley, and replace but do not lock the lid. Let the rice sit for 4 to 5 minutes, fluff with a fork, and serve.

PER SERVING: CALORIES: 174; FAT: 4G; SODIUM: 451MG; CARBOHYDRATES: 31G; FIBER: 1G; PROTEIN: 4G

Wild Rice Salad with Apples

PREP: 5 MINUTES • PRESSURE: 18 MINUTES • TOTAL: 23 MINUTES • PRESSURE LEVEL: HIGH • RELEASE: NATURAL

Ingredients
4 cups water
1¼ teaspoons kosher salt, divided
1 cup wild rice
⅓ cup walnut or olive oil
3 tablespoons cider vinegar
¼ teaspoon celery seed
⅛ teaspoon freshly ground black pepper
Pinch granulated sugar
½ cup walnut pieces, toasted
2 or 3 celery stalks, thinly sliced (about 1 cup)
1 medium Gala, Fuji, or Braeburn apple, cored and cut into ½-inch pieces

Directions
1. **Preparing the Ingredients.** Add the water into the Ninja Foodi® Multicooker ®, and 1 teaspoon of kosher salt. Stir in the wild rice.
2. **High pressure for 18 minutes.** Lock the lid on the Ninja Foodi® Multicooker and then cook for 18 minutes. To get 18-minutes cook time, press "pressure" button and use the TIME ADJUSTMENT button to adjust the cook time to 18 minutes.
3. **Pressure Release.** Use the natural-release method.
4. **Finish the dish.** Unlock and remove the lid. The rice grains should be mostly split open. If not, simmer the rice for several minutes more, in the Ninja Foodi® Multicooker set to "sauté," until at least half the grains have split. Drain and cool slightly.

   To a small jar with a tight-fitting lid, add the walnut oil, cider vinegar, celery seed, the remaining ¼ teaspoon of kosher salt, the pepper, and the sugar, and shake until well combined.

   To a medium bowl, add the cooled rice, walnuts, celery, and apple. Pour half of the dressing over the salad, and toss gently to coat, adding more dressing as desired.
5. Serve.

PER SERVING: CALORIES: 335; FAT: 17G; SODIUM: 162MG; CARBOHYDRATES: 37G; FIBER: 5G; PROTEIN: 13G

Seafood Risotto

PREP: 10 MINUTES • PRESSURE: 6 MINUTES • TOTAL: 16 MINUTES • PRESSURE LEVEL: HIGH • RELEASE: NATURAL

Ingredients

3 cups mixed seafood (shrimp, calamari, clams, etc.)
Water, as needed
2 tablespoons olive oil, plus more to finish
3 garlic cloves, chopped
3 oil-packed anchovies
2 cups Arborio or Carnaroli rice
Freshly squeezed juice of 1 lemon
2 teaspoons salt
¼ teaspoon ground white pepper
1 bunch flat-leaf parsley, chopped
Lemon wedges, for serving

Directions

1. **Preparing the Ingredients.** Separate the shellfish from the other seafood and set the shellfish aside. Add the remaining seafood to a 4-cup measuring cup and add water to just over the 4-cup mark.
   Heat the Ninja Foodi® Multicooker using the "Sauté" mode, add the oil, and heat briefly. Stir in the garlic and anchovies and sauté until the garlic is golden and the anchovies are broken up. Add the rice, stirring to coat well. While you continue to stir, look carefully at the rice, it will first become wet and look slightly transparent and pearly; then it will slowly begin to look dry and solid white again. At that point pour in the lemon juice. Scrape the bottom of the Ninja Foodi® Multicooker gently, and keep stirring until all of the juice has evaporated. Stir in the seafood and water and the salt and pepper. Place the shellfish on top without stirring any further.

2. **High pressure for 6 minutes**. Lock the lid on the Ninja Foodi® Multicooker and then cook for 6 minutes. To get 6-minutes cook time, press "pressure"button and use the TIME ADJUSTMENT button to adjust the cook time to 6 minutes.

3. **Pressure release.** When the time is up, open the Ninja Foodi® Multicooker with the Natural Release method.
   Stir the risotto. Swirl some oil over the top and sprinkle with parsley. Serve with lemon wedges.

Tiger Prawn Risotto

PREP: 10 MINUTES • PRESSURE: 30 MINUTES • TOTAL: 40 MINUTES • PRESSURE LEVEL: HIGH • RELEASE: QUICK

Ingredients

½ pound frozen tiger prawns, thawed and peeled
1 teaspoon salt
1 teaspoon white pepper
3 tablespoons olive oil
4 tablespoons butter
1 shallot, minced
3 cloves garlic, minced
2 cups Arborio rice
¾ cup cooking sake
2 teaspoons soy sauce
4 cups fish stock or Japanese Dashi
20 grams Parmesan cheese, finely grated
2 stalk green onions, thinly sliced

Directions

1. **Preparing the Ingredients.** In mixing bowl season the prawns with salt and white pepper. Set the Ninja Foodi® Multicooker on sauté, and add the olive oil and butter and sauté prawns for 5-10 minutes with the shallot and garlic, the prawns should be about 80% cooked. Remove and set aside.

   Add the Arborio rice, cooking sake, soy sauce and fish stock into Ninja Foodi® Multicooker with a swirl of olive oil. Stir and combine, make sure the rice is coated with the liquids. or Japanese Dashi

2. **High pressure for 25 minutes**. Lock the lid on the Ninja Foodi® Multicooker and then cook for 25 minutes. To get 25-minutes cook time, press "pressure" button and use the TIME ADJUSTMENT button to adjust the cook time to 25 minutes.

3. **Pressure Release.** Use the quick-release method to return the pot's pressure to normal.

   Place the prawns on top of the risotto and sprinkle the Parmesan cheese over the prawns and risotto.

4. **High pressure for 5 minutes.** Cover and lock the lid again and cook on High for another 5 minutes. To get 5-minutes cook time, press "pressure" button and use the TIME ADJUSTMENT button to adjust the cook time to 5 minutes.

5. **Pressure Release.** Use the quick-release method to return the pot's pressure to normal.

6. Garnish with the sliced green onions.

Indian Veggie Pullow

PREP: 11 MINUTES • PRESSURE: 3 MINUTES • TOTAL: 14 MINUTES • PRESSURE LEVEL: HIGH • RELEASE: NATURAL

Ingredients

- ½ cup cashews
- 2 cups basmati rice
- 4 tablespoons ghee or vegetable oil
- 1 large onion, finely chopped
- 3 cardamom pods, lightly crushed
- 3 or 4 whole cloves, lightly crushed
- 1 tablespoon smashed garlic
- 1 tablespoon peeled and grated fresh ginger
- ½ teaspoon crushed red pepper flakes
- 1 teaspoon ground coriander
- ½ teaspoon ground turmeric
- ½ teaspoon ground cinnamon
- 1 cup frozen petite green peas
- 1 cup coarsely chopped cauliflower florets (1-inch pieces)
- 2 carrots, peeled and diced
- 3 cups water
- 2 teaspoons salt

Directions

1. **Preparing the Ingredients.** Toast the cashews in a dry skillet over low heat until golden. Place the rice in a fine-mesh strainer and rinse it. Rest the strainer with the rice in a bowl and cover with water to soak.

   Meanwhile, heat the Ninja Foodi® Multicooker using the Sauté Mode, add the ghee, and heat briefly. Stir in the onion and fry until golden, about 7 minutes. Stir in the cardamom and cloves and sauté for about 1 minute. Lift the strainer so the rice can drain. Add the garlic, ginger, red pepper flakes, coriander, turmeric, and cinnamon to the onion mixture and sauté for another 30 seconds. Then add the peas, cauliflower, carrots, and rice; mix well. Sauté for about 3 more minutes. Stir in the water and salt.

2. **High pressure for 3 minutes.** Close and lock the lid of the Ninja Foodi® Multicooker. Cook at high pressure for 3 minutes. To get 3-minutes cook time, press "pressure" button and use the TIME ADJUSTMENT button to adjust the cook time to 3 minutes.

3. **Pressure Release.** When the time is up, open the Ninja Foodi® Multicooker with the 10-Minute Natural Release method.

4. **Finish the dish**. Fluff the pullow with a fork; taste and add more salt if you wish. Sprinkle the cashews over the top.

Steamed Mussels in Porter Cream Sauce

PREP: 5 MINUTES • PRESSURE: 1 MINUTES • TOTAL: 6 MINUTES • PRESSURE LEVEL: HIGH • RELEASE: QUICK

Ingredients

tablespoon olive oil

2 garlic cloves, minced

2 scallions, minced (about ⅓ cup)

1 (12-ounce) bottle porter or other dark beer

⅛ teaspoon red pepper flakes

2 pounds mussels, scrubbed and debearded

2 tablespoons heavy (whipping) cream

Directions

1. **Preparing the Ingredients.** Set the Ninja Foodi® Multicooker to "sauté," heat the olive oil until it shimmers and flows like water. Add the garlic and scallions, and cook for about 3 minutes, stirring, until the scallions just begin to brown. Pour in the beer, stirring for 1 minute, or until the foam dissipates. Add the red pepper flakes and mussels, and stir to coat with the liquid.

2. **High pressure for 1 minute.** Bring the cooker to high pressure by pressing the "pressure"button. Allow to cook for 1 minute and press Start/Stop.

3. **Pressure Release.** Use the quick-release method.

4. **Finish the dish.** Unlock and remove the lid. The mussels should be opened; if not, replace but don't lock the lid, turn the Ninja Foodi® Multicooker to "sauté"for 1 to 2 minutes more. Discard any mussels that still have not opened. Stir in the heavy cream; then pour the mussels with their sauce into a large serving bowl, and enjoy.

PER SERVING (MAIN COURSE): CALORIES: 584; FAT: 23G; SODIUM: 1,313MG; CARBOHYDRATES: 25G; FIBER:
0G; PROTEIN: 56G

Pasta with Tuna and Capers

PREP: 2 MINUTES • PRESSURE: 3 MINUTES • TOTAL: 5 MINUTES • PRESSURE LEVEL: HIGH • RELEASE: QUICK

Ingredients

- 1 tablespoon olive oil
- 1 garlic clove
- 3 anchovies
- 2 cups tomato puree
- 1½ teaspoons salt
- 16 oz. (500g) fusilli pasta
- 2 5.5oz (160g) cans Tuna packed in olive oil water to cover
- 2 tablespoons capers

Directions

1. **Preparing the Ingredients.** In the pre-heated Ninja Foodi® Multicooker on "Sauté" mode, add the oil, garlic and anchovies. Sauté until the anchovies begin to disintegrate and the garlic cloves are just starting to turn golden.

   Add the tomato puree and salt and mix together.

   Pour in the un-cooked pasta, and the contents of one tuna can (5 oz.) mixing to coat the dry pasta evenly.

   Flatten the pasta in an even layer and pour in just enough water to cover.

2. **High pressure for 3 minutes.** Lock the lid on the Ninja Foodi® Multicooker and then cook for 3 minutes. To get 3-minutes cook time, press "pressure" button and use the TIME ADJUSTMENT button to adjust the cook time to 3 minutes.

3. **Pressure release.** When time is up, open the cooker by releasing the pressure.

4. **Finish the dish.** Mix in the last 5oz of tuna and sprinkle with capers before serving. Enjoy!

Clams in White Wine

PREP: 5 MINUTES • PRESSURE: 5 MINUTES • TOTAL: 10 MINUTES • PRESSURE LEVEL: LOW• RELEASE: NATURAL

Ingredients

2 pounds live small clams, purged
1 tablespoon olive oil
3 garlic cloves, crushed
1 cup dry white wine, plus more as needed
1 small bunch flat-leaf parsley, chopped

Directions

1. **Preparing the Ingredients.** Arrange the clams in the steamer basket and set aside. Heat the Ninja Foodi® Multicooker using the "Sauté "mode, add the oil, and heat briefly. Add the garlic and sauté until it just begins to take on some color. Pour in the wine, adding enough to equal your cooker's minimum liquid requirement. Insert the steamer basket full of clams.

2. **High pressure for 5 minutes.** Close and lock the lid of the Ninja Foodi® Multicooker. Cook at low pressure for 5 minutes. To get 5-minutes cook time, press Steam button and use the TIME ADJUSTMENT button to adjust the cook time to 5 minutes

3. **Pressure Release.** When the time is up, open the Ninja Foodi® Multicooker with the Natural Release method.

4. **Finish the dish.** Invert the cooker cover on your countertop and set the steamer basket on it, shaking the basket as you lift it to allow all the clam liquid to drip down into the cooking liquid. Discard any unopened clams. Cover the steamer basket with aluminum foil and set aside to keep warm, return the cooker base to medium heat and boil the liquid until reduced by half, tumble the clams back into the Ninja Foodi® Multicooker and stir to combine well and warm through.

Spoon the clams and some sauce into individual bowls and sprinkle with the parsley. Purging Clams: Clams and other shellfish that dwell in the muddy bottom of the sea may contain a bit of sand or dirt that would not be welcome in a finished dish and so need to be purged. Mussels do not need purging as they grow on rocks or on ropes that are held vertically in the sea. To purge, place live shellfish in a very large bowl of cold saltwater (make your own using ⅓ cup of salt to a gallon of water). Let them purge for about 30 minutes, drain, and then repeat two or three times until the water is free of sand.

If not using the shellfish right away, place in a bowl, cover loosely with a damp paper towels, and refrigerate to use the next day.

Lemon and Dill Fish Packets

PREP: 10 MINUTES • PRESSURE: 5 MINUTES • TOTAL: 15 MINUTES • PRESSURE LEVEL: HIG • RELEASE: QUICK

Ingredients

  2 tilapia or cod fillets
  Salt, pepper, and garlic powder
  2 sprigs fresh dill
  4 slices lemon
  2 tablespoons butter

Directions

1. **Preparing the Ingredients.** Lay out 2 large squares of parchment paper.
   Place a fillet in the center of each parchment square, and then season with a generous amount of salt, pepper, and garlic powder.
   On each fillet, place in order: 1 sprig of dill, 2 lemon slices, and 1 tablespoon of butter.
   For best results, place a small metal rack or trivet at the bottom of your Ninja Foodi® Multicooker.
   Pour 1 cup of water into the cooker to create a water bath.
   Close up parchment paper around the fillets, folding to seal, and then place both packets on metal rack inside cooker.
2. **High pressure for 5 minutes**. Lock the lid on the Ninja Foodi® Multicooker and then cook for 5 minutes. To get 5-minutes cook time, press Steam button and use the TIME ADJUSTMENT button to adjust the cook time to 5 minutes.
3. **Pressure Release.** Perform a quick release to release the cooker's pressure. Unwrap packets and serve.
   There is no need to remove the fish from the packets before serving. In fact, it makes a really nice presentation.

Fish Filets

PREP: 5 MINUTES • PRESSURE: 12 MINUTES • TOTAL: 17 MINUTES • PRESSURE LEVEL: LOW • RELEASE: QUICK

Ingredients

4 White Fish fillets (any white fish)
1 lb. (500g) Cherry Tomatoes, halved
1 cup Black salt-cured Olives (Taggiesche, French or Kalamata)
2 Tbsp.Pickled Capers
1 bunch of fresh Thyme Olive Oil
1 clove of garlic, pressed
Salt and pepper to taste

Directions

1. **Preparing the Ingredients.** Prepare the base of the Ninja Foodi® Multicooker with 1½ to 2 cups of water and trivet or steamer basket.

   Line the bottom of the heat-proof bowl with cherry tomato halves (to keep the fish filet from sticking), add Thyme (reserve a few springs for garnish).

   Place the fish fillets over the cherry tomatoes, sprinkle with remaining tomatoes, crushed garlic, a dash of olive oil and a pinch of salt.

   Insert the dish in the Ninja Foodi® Multicooker - if your heat proof dish does not have handles construct them by making a long aluminum sling.
2. **High pressure for 5 minutes**. Lock the lid on the Ninja Foodi® Multicooker and then cook for 5 minutes. To get 5-minutes cook time, press "pressure" button and use the TIME ADJUSTMENT button to adjust the cook time to 5 minutes.
3. **Pressure Release.** Perform a quick release to release the cooker's pressure.

   Distribute fish into individual plates, top with cherry tomatoes, and sprinkle with olives, capers, fresh Thyme, a crackle of pepper and a little swirl of fresh olive oil.

Per Serving Calories: 278.2; Fat: 5.8g; Carbohydrates: 18.8g; Sodium: 1056.8mg; Fiber: 2.5g; Protien: 25.6g

Mediterranean Tuna Noodle Delight

PREP: 6 MINUTES • PRESSURE: 10 MINUTES • TOTAL: 16 MINUTES • PRESSURE LEVEL: HIGH • RELEASE: NATURAL

Ingredients
- 1 Tablespoon of Oil
- ½ cup of chopped red onion
- 8 ounces of dry wide egg noodles (uncooked)
- 1 can (14 ounces) diced tomatoes with basil, garlic and oregano(undrained) or any kind you have on hand.
- 1-1/4 cups of water
- ¼ teaspoon of salt
- 1/8 teaspoon of pepper
- 1 can of tuna fish in water, drained
- 1 jar (7.5 oz.) marinated artichoke hearts, drained with saving the liquid, then chop it up
- Crumpled feta cheese
- Fresh chopped parsley or dried

Directions
1. **Preparing the Ingredients.** Sauté the red onion for about 2 minutes.
   Add the dry noodles, tomatoes, water, salt and pepper .
2. **High pressure for 10 minutes.** Lock the lid on the Ninja Foodi® Multicooker and then cook for 10 minutes. To get 10-minutes cook time, press "pressure" button and adjust the time.
3. **Pressure Release.** Release the pressure using natural release method.
   Turn off the warm setting.
   Add tuna, artichokes and your reserved liquid from the artichokes and sauté on normal while stirring for about 4 more minutes till hot.
   Plate, then top with a little feta cheese and parsley to your liking.

Per Serving Calories: 258.3; Fat: 5.8g; Carbohydrates: 15.8g; Sugar: 0.2g; Sodium: 1146.8mg; Fiber: 2.5g; Protien: 29.6g

Quick Seafood Paella

PREP: 10 MINUTES • PRESSURE: 25 MINUTES • TOTAL: 35 MINUTES • PRESSURE LEVEL: HIGH • RELEASE: NATURAL

Ingredients

- 4 white fish heads
- 2 carrots
- 1 Celery
- 1 Bay leaf
- Bunch of parsley with stems
- 6 Cups of water
- 4 Tbsp. EVOO
- 1 Medium Yellow Onion, diced
- 1 Red Bell Pepper - diced
- 1 Green Bell Pepper - diced
- Large pinch saffron threads
- 2 Cups short-grain rice
- 1¾ Cups Vegetable Stock or Seafood Stock
- ⅛ Tsp Ground Turmeric
- 2 Tsp Sea Salt
- 1 Cup of seafood (squid, meaty white fish, scallops)
- 2 Cups of mixed shellfish (clams, mussels, shrimp)

Directions

1. **Preparing the Ingredients.** Add all the ingredients to Ninja Foodi® Multicooker. Set on High for 5 minutes. When timer goes off, use Natural-release.
   Set Ninja Foodi® Multicooker on "Sauté" and heat EVOO.
   When the oil gets hot, add onions and peppers and Sauté until onions soften, about 4 minutes.
   Stir in the saffron, rice, and seafood and sauté everything together for 2 minutes.
   Then add stock, turmeric, salt, and mix well.
   Arrange the shellfish on top and do not mix further.
2. **High pressure for 6 minutes** Close and lock the lid of the Ninja Foodi® Multicooker. Cook at High pressure for 6 minutes. To get 6-minutes cook time, press "pressure" button and use the TIME ADJUSTMENT button to adjust the cook time to 6 minutes.
3. **Pressure Release.** When timer is up, use natural pressure release method.
4. **Finish the dish.** Open the lid when the vent valve opens and mix the paella well, cover and let stand for 1 minute before serving.

Serve and Enjoy!

Steamed Salmon With Garlic-Citrus

PREP: 5 MINUTES • PRESSURE: 6 MINUTES • TOTAL: 10 MINUTES • PRESSURE: HIGH • RELEASE: QUICK

Ingredients

4 tablespoons (½ stick) unsalted butter, at room temperature
2 teaspoons minced garlic
1 teaspoon finely grated orange zest
1 teaspoon finely grated lemon zest
½ teaspoon salt
½ teaspoon ground black pepper
Two 1-pound skin-on salmon fillets

Directions

1. **Preparing the Ingredients**. Mash the butter, garlic, both zests, salt, and pepper in a small bowl until uniform.
   Pour 2 cups water in the Ninja Foodi® Multicooker. Line a large steamer basket with parchment paper; set it in the cooker. Add the fillets skin side down; top with the butter mixture.
2. **High pressure for 6 minutes.** Lock the lid onto the pot. Set the Ninja Foodi® Multicooker to cook at high pressure for 6 minutes. To get 6-minutes cook time, press "pressure" button and use the TIME ADJUSTMENT button to adjust the cook time to 6 minutes.
3. **Pressure Release.** Use the quick-release method to drop the pot's pressure to normal.
4. **Finish the dish.** Unlock and open the pot. Transfer the salmon to a large platter and slice each fillet into two or three pieces to serve.

Fish *and* Vegetable "Tagine" *with* Chermoula

PREP: 5 MINUTES • PRESSURE: 5 MINUTES • TOTAL: 10 MINUTES • PRESSURE LEVEL: HIGH • RELEASE: NATURAL

Ingredients
- For The Chermoula
  4 large garlic cloves
  1 cup fresh cilantro leaves
  1 cup fresh parsley leaves
  ¼ cup freshly squeezed lemon juice (about 2 lemons)
  1½ teaspoons kosher salt
  1 heaping teaspoon ground sweet paprika
  ¼ teaspoon ground cumin
  ¼ teaspoon ground cayenne pepper
  2 tablespoons olive oil
- For The Fish And Vegetables
  2 (7-ounce) tilapia fillets
  ¼ teaspoon kosher salt
  10 ounces Yukon gold potatoes (about 2 medium or 3 small), peeled and sliced ¼ inch thick
  ½ medium red bell pepper, cut into bite-size chunks
  ½ medium green bell pepper, cut into bite-size chunks
  1 very small onion, sliced
  ¼ cup water
  1 large tomato, seeded and diced

To make the chermoula
1. **Preparing the Ingredients.** Into the chute of a small running food processor, drop the garlic cloves, one at a time, and process until minced. Add the cilantro, parsley, lemon juice, kosher salt, paprika, cumin, and cayenne pepper, and process until mostly smooth. With the processor still running, slowly drizzle in the olive oil, and process until the sauce is emulsified.

   If you don't have a food processor, finely mince the garlic, cilantro, and parsley. Transfer to a small bowl, and stir in the lemon juice, kosher salt, paprika, cumin, and cayenne pepper. Slowly whisk in the olive oil. The sauce won't be as smooth as if prepared in a food processor, but it will taste good.

To make the fish and vegetables
1. **Preparing the Ingredients.** Sprinkle both sides of the fish fillets lightly with the kosher salt, and brush with 3 tablespoons of chermoula. Refrigerate the fish.

Add the potato slices, red bell pepper, green bell pepper, and onion. Pour in ⅓ cup of chermoula, and gently toss the vegetables to coat. Pour the water over the vegetables.

2. **High pressure for 5 minutes.** Lock the lid on the Ninja Foodi® Multicooker and then cook for 5 minutes. To get 5-minutes cook time, press "pressure" button and use the TIME ADJUSTMENT button to adjust the cook time to 5 minutes.

3. **Pressure release.** Use the quick-release method.

   Unlock and remove the lid. Sprinkle the tomato over the vegetables in the Ninja Foodi® Multicooker, and lay the fillets on top. Drizzle with the remaining chermoula.

4. **High pressure for 1 minute.** Lock the lid in place again; bring the cooker to high pressure by pressing "pressure" button. Allow to cook for 1 minute and press KEEP WARM/CANCEL.

   When the timer goes off, turn the cooker off. ("Warm" setting, turn off).

5. **Pressure release.** After cooking, use the natural method to release pressure for 4 minutes, then the quick method to release the remaining pressure.

6. **Finish the dish.** Unlock and remove the lid. Using a large spatula, carefully remove the fish fillets and vegetables and divide them between 2 plates. Spoon any residual sauce over the fish, and serve.

PER SERVING: CALORIES: 479; FAT: 17G; SODIUM: 2,157MG; CARBOHYDRATES: 43G; FIBER: 7G; PROTEIN: 44G

Coconut Fish Curry

PREP: 5 MINUTES • PRESSURE: 15 MINUTES • TOTAL: 20 MINUTES • PRESSURE LEVEL: HIGH • RELEASE: QUICK

Ingredients

- 1-1.5 lb. (500-750g) Fish steaks or fillets, rinsed and cut into bite-size pieces (fresh or frozen and thawed)
- 1 Tomato, chopped (or a heaping cup of cherry tomatoes)
- 2 Green Chiles, sliced into strips
- 2 Medium onions, sliced into strips
- 2 Garlic cloves, squeezed
- 1 Tbsp. freshly grated Ginger, or ⅛ tsp. Ginger Powder
- 6 Curry leaves, or Bay Laurel Leaves, or Kaffir Lime Leaves, or Basil
- 1 Tbsp. ground Coriander
- 2 tsp. ground Cumin
- ½ tsp. ground Turmeric
- 1 tsp. Chili Powder , or 1 tsp. of Hot Pepper Flakes
- ½ tsp. Ground Fenugreek (Methi)
- 3 Tbsp. of Curry Powder mix. (instead of the 5 spices noted above)
- 2 cups or (500ml) un-sweetened Coconut Milk
- Salt to taste (I used about 2 tsp.)
- Lemon juice to taste (I used the juice from ½ lemon)

Directions

1. **Preparing the Ingredients.** In the preheated Ninja Foodi® Multicooker, add a swirl of oil and then drop in the curry leaves and lightly fry them until golden around the edges (about 1 minute).

   Then add the onion, garlic and ginger and Sauté until the onion is soft.

   Add all of the ground spices: Coriander, Cumin, Turmeric, Chili Powder and Fenugreek and Sauté them together with the onions until they have released their aroma (about 2 minutes).

   De-glaze with the coconut milk making sure to un-stick anything from the bottom of the cooker and incorporate it in the sauce.

   Add the Green Chiles, Tomatoes and fish pieces. Stir to coat the fish well with the mixture.

2. **High pressure for 3 minutes.** Lock the lid on the Ninja Foodi® Multicooker and then cook for 3 minutes. To get 3-minutes cook time, press "pressure" button and use the TIME ADJUSTMENT button to adjust the cook time to 3 minutes.

3. **Pressure Release.** Use the "Quick Release" method to vent the steam, then open the lid.

4. **Finish the dish.** Add salt to taste and spritz with lemon juice just before serving. Serve alone, or with steamed rice.

Main Dishes – Vegetables

Curried Cauliflower

PREP: 5 MINUTES • PRESSURE: 7 MINUTES • TOTAL: 12 MINUTES • PRESSURE LEVEL: HIGH • RELEASE: QUICK

Ingredients

½ cup white wine
1 cup Chicken Stock or low-sodium broth
2 tablespoons unsalted butter or olive oil
2 teaspoons curry powder
2 teaspoons kosher salt
1 whole head cauliflower, base trimmed flat and any leaves removed

Directions

1. **Preparing the Ingredients.** Turn the Ninja Foodi® Multicooker to "sauté," pour in the white wine and Chicken Stock. Add the butter, curry powder, and kosher salt. Simmer for about 1 minute, or until the butter just melts and is incorporated into the sauce. Add the cauliflower.

2. **High pressure for 7 minutes.** Lock the lid in place, and bring the pot to high pressure. Cook at high pressure for 7 minutes. To get 7minutes cook time, press "pressure"button and use the TIME ADJUSTMENT button to adjust the cook time to 7 minutes.

3. **Pressure Release.** Use the quick-release method.

4. **Finish the dish.** Unlock and remove the lid. Using two large forks or slotted spatulas, transfer the cauliflower to a cutting board.
   Turn the Ninja Foodi® Multicooker to "sauté." Simmer the sauce for about 6 minutes, or until reduced by about two-thirds.
   Meanwhile, break the cauliflower into florets. Discard the core. When the sauce has reduced to the desired consistency, add the cauliflower, toss to coat, and serve.
   If you are a fan of mashed cauliflower, cook the whole cauliflower for 15 minutes on high pressure with a quick release for cauliflower so soft it will practically mash itself. Reduce the sauce by about half, and then mash the cauliflower into it, adding more broth or butter as desired.

PER SERVING: CALORIES: 144; FAT: 7G; SODIUM: 373MG; CARBOHYDRATES: 13G; FIBER: 6G; PROTEIN: 5G

Air Fryer Asparagus

PREP: 5 MINUTES • COOK TIME: 8 MINUTES • TOTAL: 13 MINUTES
SERVES: 2

Ingredients

Nutritional yeast

Olive oil non-stick spray
One bunch of asparagus

Directions

1. **Preparing the Ingredients.** Wash asparagus and then trim off thick, woody ends. Spray asparagus with olive oil spray and sprinkle with yeast.
2. **Air Frying.** In your air fryer, lay asparagus in a singular layer. Close crisping lid. Select AIR CRISP, set temperatura to 360°F, and set time to 8 minutes. Select START/STOP to begin.

PER SERVING: CALORIES: 17; FAT: 4G; PROTEIN: 9G

Spicy Sweet Potato Fries

PREP: 5 MINUTES • COOK TIME: 37 MINUTES • TOTAL: 45 MINUTES
SERVES: 2

Ingredients

1 tbsp. sweet potato fry seasoning mix

1 tbsp. olive oil

2 sweet potatoes

Seasoning Mix:

2 tbsp. salt

1 tbsp. cayenne pepper

1 tbsp. dried oregano

1 tbsp. fennel

2 tbsp. coriander

Directions:

1. **Preparing the Ingredients.** Slice both ends off sweet potatoes and peel. Slice lengthwise in half and again crosswise to make four pieces from each potato.
   Slice each potato piece into 2-3 slices, then slice into fries.
   Grind together all of seasoning mix ingredients and mix in the salt.
   Ensure air fryer is preheated to 350 degrees.
   Toss potato pieces in olive oil, sprinkling with seasoning mix and tossing well to coat thoroughly.

2. **Air Frying.** Add fries to air fryer basket. Close crisping lid. Select AIR CRISP, set temperatura to 350°F, and set time to 27 minutes. Select START/STOP to begin.
   Take out the basket and turn fries. Turn off air fryer and let cook 10-12 minutes till fries are golden.

PER SERVING: CALORIES: 89; FAT: 14G; PROTEIN: 8Gs; SUGAR:3G

Air Fryer Cauliflower Rice

PREP: 5 MINUTES • COOK TIME: 20 MINUTES • TOTAL: 25 MINUTES

SERVES: 2

Ingredients

Round 1:

1tsp. turmeric

1 C. diced carrot

½ C. diced onion

2 tbsp. low-sodium soy sauce

½ block of extra firm tofu

Round 2:

½ C. frozen peas

2 minced garlic cloves

½ C. chopped broccoli

1 tbsp. minced ginger

1 tbsp. rice vinegar

1 ½ tsp. toasted sesame oil

2 tbsp. reduced-sodium soy sauce

3 C. riced cauliflower

Directions:

1 **Preparing the Ingredients.** Crumble tofu in a large bowl and toss with all the Round one ingredients.

2 **Air Frying.** Preheat air fryer to 370 degrees, close crisping lid. Select AIR CRISP, set temperatura to 370°F, and set time to 10 minutes. Select START/STOP to begin and cook 10 minutes, making sure to shake once.

In another bowl, toss ingredients from Round 2 together.

Add Round 2 mixture to air fryer and cook another 10 minutes, ensuring to shake 5 minutes in.

Enjoy!

PER SERVING: CALORIES: 67; FAT: 8G; PROTEIN: 3G; SUGAR:0G

Air Fried Carrots, Yellow Squash & Zucchini

PREP: 5 MINUTES • COOK TIME: 35 MINUTES • TOTAL: 40 MINUTES

SERVES: 2

Ingredients

1 tbsp. chopped tarragon leaves
½ tsp. white pepper
1 tsp. salt
½ pound yellow squash
½ pound zucchini
6 tsp. olive oil
½ pound carrots

Directions:

1   **Preparing the Ingredients.** Stem and root the end of squash and zucchini and cut in ¾-inch half-moons. Peel and cut carrots into 1-inch cubes

  Combine carrot cubes with 2 teaspoons of olive oil, tossing to combine.

2   **Air Frying.** Pour into air fryer basket, close crisping lid. Select AIR CRISP, set temperatura to 400°F, and set time to 5 minutes. Select START/STOP to begin and cook.

  As carrots cook, drizzle remaining olive oil over squash and zucchini pieces, then season with pepper and salt. Toss well to coat.

  Add squash and zucchini when the timer for carrots goes off. Cook 30 minutes, making sure to toss 2-3 times during the cooking process.

  Once done, take out veggies and toss with tarragon. Serve up warm!

PER SERVING: CALORIES: 122; FAT: 9G; PROTEIN: 6G; SUGAR:0G

Zucchini Parmesan Chips

PREP: 10 MINUTES • COOK TIME: 8 MINUTES • TOTAL: 18 MINUTES
SERVES: 10

Ingredients
½ tsp. paprika
½ C. grated parmesan cheese
½ C. Italian breadcrumbs
1 lightly beaten egg
1 thinly sliced zucchini

Directions:

1 **Preparing the Ingredients.** Use a very sharp knife or mandolin slicer to slice zucchini as thinly as you can. Pat off extra moisture.

   Beat egg with a pinch of pepper and salt and a bit of water.

   Combine paprika, cheese, and breadcrumbs in a bowl.

   Dip slices of zucchini into the egg mixture and then into breadcrumb mixture. Press gently to coat.

2 **Air Frying**. With olive oil cooking spray, mist coated zucchini slices. Place into your air fryer in a single layer. Close crisping lid. Select AIR CRISP, set temperature to 350°F, and set time to 8 minutes. Select START/STOP to begin.

   Sprinkle with salt and serve with salsa.

PER SERVING: CALORIES: 211; FAT: 16G; PROTEIN:8G; SUGAR:0G

Crispy Roasted Broccoli

PREP: 10 MINUTES • COOK TIME: 8 MINUTES • TOTAL: 18 MINUTES

SERVES: 2

Ingredients

¼ tsp. Masala
½ tsp. red chili powder
½ tsp. salt
¼ tsp. turmeric powder
1 tbsp. chickpea flour
2 tbsp. yogurt
1 pound broccoli

Directions:

1 **Preparing the Ingredients.** Cut broccoli up into florets. Soak in a bowl of water with 2 teaspoons of salt for at least half an hour to remove impurities.

   Take out broccoli florets from water and let drain. Wipe down thoroughly.

   Mix all other ingredients together to create a marinade.

   Toss broccoli florets in the marinade. Cover and chill 15-30 minutes.

2 **Air Frying.** Preheat air fryer to 390 degrees. Place marinated broccoli florets into the fryer. Close crisping lid. Select AIR CRISP, set temperature to 350°F, and set time to 10 minutes. Select START/STOP to begin. Florets will be crispy when done.

PER SERVING: CALORIES: 96; FAT: 1.3G; PROTEIN:7G; SUGAR:4.5G

Crispy Jalapeno Coins

PREP: 10 MINUTES • COOK TIME: 5 MINUTES • TOTAL: 15 MINUTES

SERVES: 2

Ingredients

1 egg
2-3 tbsp. coconut flour
1 sliced and seeded jalapeno
Pinch of garlic powder
Pinch of onion powder
Pinch of Cajun seasoning (optional)
Pinch of pepper and salt

Directions:

1 **Preparing the Ingredients.** Ensure your air fryer is preheated to 400 degrees.

   Mix together all dry ingredients.

   Pat jalapeno slices dry. Dip coins into egg wash and then into dry mixture. Toss to thoroughly coat.

   Add coated jalapeno slices to air fryer in a singular layer. Spray with olive oil.

2 **Air Frying.** Close crisping lid. Select AIR CRISP, set temperature to 350°F, and set time to 5 minutes. Select START/STOP to begin. Cook just till crispy.

PER SERVING: CALORIES: 128; FAT: 8G; PROTEIN:7G; SUGAR:0G

Buffalo Cauliflower

PREP: 5 MINUTES • COOK TIME: 15 MINUTES • TOTAL: 20 MINUTES
SERVES: 2

Ingredients

Cauliflower:
1 C. panko breadcrumbs
1 tsp. salt
4 C. cauliflower florets
Buffalo Coating:
¼ C. Vegan Buffalo sauce
¼ C. melted vegan butter

Directions:

1 **Preparing the Ingredients.** Melt butter in microwave and whisk in buffalo sauce.
   Dip each cauliflower floret into buffalo mixture, ensuring it gets coated well. Hold over a
   bowl till floret is done dripping.
   Mix breadcrumbs with salt.

2 **Air Frying.** Dredge dipped florets into breadcrumbs and place into air fryer. Close
   crisping lid. Select AIR CRISP, set temperature to 350°F, and set time to 15 minutes.
   Select START/STOP to begin. When slightly browned, they are ready to eat!
   Serve with your favorite keto dipping sauce!

PER SERVING: CALORIES: 194; FAT: 17G; PROTEIN:10G; SUGAR:3G

Cinnamon Butternut Squash Fries

PREP: 5 MINUTES • COOK TIME: 10 MINUTES • TOTAL: 15 MINUTES
SERVES: 2

Ingredients
1 pinch of salt
1 tbsp. powdered unprocessed sugar
½ tsp. nutmeg
1 tsp. cinnamon
1 tbsp. coconut oil
4 ounces pre-cut butternut squash fries

Directions:
1 **Preparing the Ingredients.** In a plastic bag, pour in all ingredients. Coat fries with other components till coated and sugar is dissolved.
2 **Air Frying.** Spread coated fries into a single layer in the air fryer. Close crisping lid. Select AIR CRISP, set temperature to 390°F, and set time to 10 minutes. Select START/STOP to begin. Cook until crispy.

PER SERVING: CALORIES: 175; FAT: 8G; PROTEIN:1G; SUGAR:0G

Buttered Brussels Sprouts

PREP: 5 MINUTES • PRESSURE: 3 MINUTES • TOTAL: 8 MINUTES • PRESSURE LEVEL: HIGH • RELEASE: NATURAL

Ingredients

Brussels sprouts does not exceed two-thirds of the cooker's capacity.

1 pound Brussels sprouts

½ teaspoon salt, plus more if desired

1 tablespoon unsalted butter, diced, at room temperature

1 tablespoon grated orange zest

Freshly ground black pepper

Directions

1. **Preparing the Ingredients.** Add 1 cup of water (or the minimum amount required by your cooker to reach pressure) to the Ninja Foodi® Multicooker base. To ensure even cooking, cut any large sprouts in half from top to bottom. Place the sprouts in the steamer basket in an even layer and lower it into the cooker; sprinkle with ½ teaspoon salt.
2. **High pressure for 3 minutes.** Close and lock the lid of the Ninja Foodi® Multicooker. Cook at high pressure for 3 minutes, To get 3 minutes cook time, press "pressure" button and use the TIME ADJUSTMENT button to adjust the cook time to 3 minutes.
3. **Pressure Release.**When the time is up, open the cooker with the natural release method.
4. **Finish the dish.** Lift the steamer basket out of the cooker and immediately tumble the sprouts into a serving dish to keep them from overcooking. Toss with the butter and orange zest and season with pepper and more salt if you wish.

Ratatouille

PREP: 5 MINUTES • PRESSURE: 4 MINUTES • TOTAL: 9 MINUTES • PRESSURE LEVEL: HIGH • RELEASE: QUICK

Ingredients

- Kosher salt, for salting and seasoning
- 1 small eggplant, peeled and sliced ½ inch thick
- 1 medium zucchini, sliced ½ inch thick
- 2 tablespoons olive oil
- 1 cup chopped onion
- 3 garlic cloves, minced or pressed
- 1 small green bell pepper, cut into ½-inch chunks (about 1 cup)
- 1 small red bell pepper, cut into ½-inch chunks (about 1 cup)
- 1 rib celery, sliced (about 1 cup)
- 1 (14.5-ounce) can diced tomatoes, undrained
- ¼ cup water
- ½ teaspoon dried oregano
- ¼ teaspoon freshly ground black pepper
- 2 tablespoons minced fresh basil
- ¼ cup pitted green or black olives (optional)

Directions

1. **Preparing the Ingredients.** Place a rack over a baking sheet. With kosher salt, very liberally salt one side of the eggplant and zucchini slices, and place them, salted-side down, on the rack. Salt the other side. Let the slices sit for 15 to 20 minutes, or until they start to exude water (you'll see it beading up on the surface of the slices and dripping into the sheet pan). Rinse the slices, and blot them dry. Cut the zucchini slices into quarters and the eggplant slices into eighths.

   Turn the Ninja Foodi® Multicooker to "sauté," heat the olive oil until it shimmers and flows like water. Add the onion and garlic, and sprinkle with a pinch or two of kosher salt. Cook for about 3 minutes, stirring, until the onions just begin to brown.

   Add the eggplant, zucchini, green bell pepper, red bell pepper, celery, and tomatoes with their juice, water, and oregano.

2. **High pressure for 4 minutes.** Lock the lid on the Ninja Foodi® Multicooker and then cook for 4 minutes. To get 4-minutes cook time, press "pressure" button and use the TIME ADJUSTMENT button to adjust the cook time to 4 minutes.

3. **Pressure Release.** Use the quick-release method.

4. **Finish the dish.** Unlock and remove the lid. Stir in the pepper, basil, and olives (if using). Taste, adjust the seasoning as needed, and serve.

While this vegetable dish is usually served on its own, it's great tossed with cooked pasta or served over polenta.

PER SERVING: CALORIES: 149; FAT: 8G; SODIUM: 55MG; CARBOHYDRATES: 20G; FIBER: 8G; PROTEIN: 4G

Beets *and* Greens *with* Horseradish Sauce

PREP: 5 MINUTES • PRESSURE: 10 MINUTES • TOTAL: 15 MINUTES • PRESSURE LEVEL: HIGH • RELEASE: NATURAL

Ingredients

   2 large or 3 small beets with greens, scrubbed and root ends trimmed
   1 cup water, for steaming
   2 tablespoons sour cream
   1 tablespoon whole milk
   1 teaspoon prepared horseradish
   ¼ teaspoon lemon zest
   ⅛ teaspoon kosher salt, divided
   2 teaspoons unsalted butter
   1 tablespoon minced fresh chives

Directions

1. **Preparing the Ingredients.** Trim off the beet greens and set aside. If the beets are very large (3 inches or more in diameter), quarter them; otherwise, halve them. Add the water and insert the steamer basket or trivet. Place the beets on the steamer insert.

2. **High pressure for 10 minutes.** Lock the lid on the Ninja Foodi® Multicooker and then cook for 10 minutes. To get 10-minutes cook time, press "pressure" button. When the timer goes off, turn the cooker off. ("Warm" setting, turn off).

3. **Pressure release.** Let the pressure to come down naturally .

   While the beets are cooking and the pressure is releasing, wash the greens and slice them into ½-inch-thick ribbons, removing any tough stems. In a small bowl, whisk together the sour cream, milk, horseradish, lemon zest, and $1/16$ teaspoon of kosher salt.

4. **Finish the dish.** When the pressure has released completely, unlock and remove the lid. Remove the beets and cool slightly; then use a paring knife or peeler to peel them. Slice them into large bite-size pieces and set aside.
   Remove the steamer from the Ninja Foodi® Multicooker, and pour out the water. Turn the Ninja Foodi® Multicooker to "brown.".Add the butter to melt. When the butter stops foaming, add the beet greens and sprinkle with the remaining $1/16$ teaspoon of kosher salt. Cook for 3 to 4 minutes, stirring, until wilted. Return the beets to the Ninja Foodi® Multicooker and heat for 1 or 2 minutes, stirring. Transfer the beets and greens to a platter, and drizzle with the sour cream mixture. Sprinkle with the chives, and serve.

It may be tempting to cool the beets completely before you peel them, but that would be a mistake. Beets are easiest to peel when they're just cool enough to handle; if they get too cool, the skins tend to stick.

PER SERVING: CALORIES: 70; FAT: 4G; SODIUM: 162MG; CARBOHYDRATES: 9G; FIBER: 2G; PROTEIN: 2G

Carrots Escabeche

PREP: 5 MINUTES • PRESSURE: 2 MINUTES • TOTAL: 7 MINUTES • PRESSURE LEVEL: HIGH • RELEASE: QUICK

Ingredients

1 pound carrots, peeled and cut into ½-inch-thick slices
¼ cup white wine vinegar
⅓ cup olive oil
½ teaspoon kosher salt
3 tablespoons chopped fresh cilantro
2 tablespoons chopped fresh flat-leaf parsley
2 teaspoons chopped fresh mint
1 garlic clove, minced

Directions

1. **Preparing the Ingredients.** In the Ninja Foodi® Multicooker, place the carrots, and pour in enough water to cover them.
2. **High pressure for 3 minutes.** Lock the lid in place, and bring the pot to high pressure. Cook at high pressure for 3 minutes. To get 3-minutes cook time, press "pressure" button and use the TIME ADJUSTMENT button to adjust the cook time to 3 minutes.
3. **Pressure Release.** Use the quick-release method.
4. **Finish the dish.** Drain the carrots, and transfer them to a medium bowl. In a small bowl, whisk together the white wine vinegar, olive oil, and kosher salt. Pour the mixture over the hot carrots, and stir gently. Cool the carrots to room temperature, then add the cilantro, parsley, mint, and garlic. Stir gently to combine. Serve slightly chilled or at room temperature.

PER SERVING: CALORIES: 232; FAT: 21G; SODIUM: 371MG; CARBOHYDRATES: 12G; FIBER: 3G; PROTEIN: 1G

Braised Red Cabbage With Apples

PREP: 5 MINUTES • PRESSURE: 13 MINUTES • TOTAL: 18 MINUTES • PRESSURE LEVEL: HIGH • RELEASE: QUICK

Ingredients
4 thin bacon slices, chopped
1 small red onion, chopped
1 medium tart green apple, such as Granny Smith, peeled, cored, and chopped
1 teaspoon dried thyme
¼ teaspoon ground allspice
¼ teaspoon ground mace
1 tablespoon packed dark brown sugar
1 tablespoon balsamic vinegar
1 medium red cabbage (about 2 pounds), cored and thinly sliced
½ cup chicken broth

Directions
1. **Preparing the Ingredients.** Fry the bacon in the Ninja Foodi® Multicooker turned to the "sauté" function, stirring often, until crisp, about 4 minutes.
   Add the onion to the pot; cook, stirring often, until soft, about 4 minutes. Add the apple, thyme, allspice, and mace. Cook about 1 minute, stirring all the while, until fragrant. Stir in the brown sugar and vinegar; keep stirring until bubbling, about 1 minute.
   Add the cabbage; toss well to mix evenly with the other ingredients. Drizzle the broth over the cabbage mixture.
2. **High pressure for 13 minutes.** Lock the lid on the Ninja Foodi® Multicooker and then cook for 13 minutes. To get 13-minutes cook time, press "pressure" button, and use the TIME ADJUSTMENT button to adjust the cook time to 13 minutes.
3. **Pressure Release.** Use the quick-release method to return the pot to normal pressure. Unlock and open the pot. Stir well before serving.

Vinegary Collard Greens

PREP: 5 MINUTES • PRESSURE: 6 MINUTES • TOTAL: 11 MINUTES • PRESSURE LEVEL: HIGH • RELEASE: QUICK

Ingredients

4 ounces slab bacon, diced
1 small yellow onion, chopped
2 teaspoons minced garlic
1½ pounds collard greens, tough stems removed and the leaves chopped (about 8 packed cups)
½ cup chicken broth
3 tablespoons balsamic vinegar
2 tablespoons canned tomato paste
1 tablespoon packed dark brown sugar

Directions

1. **Preparing the Ingredients.** Put the bacon in the Ninja Foodi® Multicooker turned to the "Sauté" function; fry until crisp and well browned, stirring occasionally, about 4 minutes.
Add the onion; cook, stirring often, until translucent, about 2 minutes. Add the garlic, stir well, and add the collard greens. Stir over the heat for 2 minutes, then pour in the broth, vinegar, tomato paste, and brown sugar until the latter two items dissolve into the sauce. Stir well one more time.
2. **High pressure for 6 minutes** Lock the lid onto the pot. Set the Ninja Foodi® Multicooker to cook at high pressure for 6 minutes. To get 6-minutes cook time, press "pressure" button, and use the TIME ADJUSTMENT button to adjust the cook time to 6 minutes.
3. **Pressure Release.** Use the quick-release method.
4. **Finish the dish**. Unlock and open the pot. Stir well before serving.

Braised Celery *and* Tomatoes

PREP: 5 MINUTES • PRESSURE: 12 MINUTES • TOTAL: 17 MINUTES • PRESSURE LEVEL: HIGH • RELEASE: QUICK

Ingredients

1-teaspoon olive oil

3 bacon slices, diced (about ½ cup)

2 cups thinly sliced onion

½ teaspoon kosher salt, plus additional for seasoning

1 (1-pound) celery bunch, cut into 1-inch pieces (about 4 cups)

⅓ cup dry white wine

1 (14.5-ounce) can diced tomatoes, drained

Freshly ground black pepper

½ cup pale yellow celery leaves, roughly chopped (optional)

Directions

1. **Preparing the Ingredients.** Turn the Ninja Foodi® Multicooker to "sauté," add the olive oil and bacon. Cook for about 3 minutes, stirring, until the bacon has released most of its fat and just begun to brown. Add the onion, and sprinkle with ½ teaspoon of kosher salt. Cook for about 2 minutes, stirring, until the onions begin to soften; then add the celery. Stir to coat the celery with the bacon fat. Add the white wine and tomatoes.

2. **High pressure for 12 minutes.** Lock the lid in place, and bring the pot to high pressure.
Cook at high pressure for 12 minutes. To get 12-minutes cook time, press "pressure" button and adjust the time.

3. **Pressure Release.** Use the quick-release method.

4. **Finish the dish.** Unlock and remove the lid. If there is a lot of liquid in the Ninja Foodi® Multicooker, turn the Ninja Foodi® Multicooker to "sauté," and simmer until most of the liquid is gone. Season to taste with a few grinds of pepper and additional salt, if necessary. Garnish with the celery leaves (if using), and serve.

5. This dish works best with the larger, outer celery stalks. Reserve the small, pale inside stalks for another use. One large bunch of celery should provide the 4 cups called for in this recipe.

PER SERVING: CALORIES: 114; FAT: 4G; SODIUM: 248MG; CARBOHYDRATES: 13G; FIBER: 4G; PROTEIN: 4G.

Roasted Rainbow Fingerling Potatoes

PREP: 5 MINUTES • PRESSURE: 20 MINUTES • TOTAL: 25 MINUTES • PRESSURE LEVEL: HIGH • RELEASE: QUICK

Ingredients

- ½ cup (100 g) diced onion
- 2 tbsp. (30 ml) ghee
- 1 tbsp. (15 ml) olive oil
- 2 lb. (907 g) rainbow fingerling potatoes
- Up to 1 tsp (5 g) sea salt
- ¼ tsp black pepper
- ½ tsp onion powder
- ½ tsp paprika

Directions

1. **Preparing the Ingredients.** Begin by sautéing the onion in your Ninja Foodi® Multicooker in the ghee and olive oil for 5 minutes.
   Add in the potatoes and seasonings and secure the lid.
2. **High pressure for 20 minutes.** Lock the lid on the Ninja Foodi® Multicooker and then cook for 20 minutes. To get 20-minutes cook time, press "pressure" button and use the TIME ADJUSTMENT button to adjust the cook time to 20 minutes.
3. **Pressure Release.** Quick-release the pressure valve when complete and carefully remove the lid.
4. Serve warm.

Main Dishes – Desserts

Chocolate Brownie

PREP: 5 MINUTES • PRESSURE: 15 MINUTES • TOTAL: 20 MINUTES • PRESSURE LEVEL: HIGH • RELEASE: QUICK

Ingredients

2 tablespoons unsalted butter

1 tablespoon dark chocolate chips

⅓ cup granulated sugar

1 egg

⅛ teaspoon vanilla extract

¼ cup all-purpose flour

2 tablespoons cocoa powder

1 cup water, for steaming (double-check the Ninja Foodi® Multicooker manual to confirm amount, and follow the manual if there is a discrepancy)

1 tablespoon confectioners' sugar or powdered sugar

Directions

1. **Preparing the Ingredients.** In a small microwave-safe bowl, microwave the butter and chocolate chips for 30 seconds on high to melt. Into a small mixing bowl, scrape the chocolate mixture, and add the sugar. Beat for about 2 minutes. Add the egg and vanilla, and beat for about 1 minute more, until smooth. Sift the flour and cocoa powder over the wet ingredients, and beat until just combined.

   Spoon the batter into a nonstick mini springform pan (4½ inches) or a mini loaf pan (3-by-5-inch), and smooth the top.

   Add the water into the Ninja Foodi® Multicooker, and insert the steamer basket or trivet. Place the loaf pan on the steamer insert. Place a square of aluminum foil over the pan, but don't crimp it down; it's just to keep steam from condensing on the surface of the cake.

2. **High pressure for 15 minutes.** Lock the lid in place, and bring the pot to high pressure.

   Cook at high pressure for 15 minutes. To get 15-minutes cook time, press "pressure"button and adjust the time.

3. **Pressure Release.** Use the quick-release method.

4. **Finish the dish.** Unlock and remove the lid. Using tongs, remove the sheet of foil. Transfer the pan to a cutting board or rack to cool. Dust the cake with the confectioners' sugar, slice, and serve.

PER SERVING: CALORIES: 370; FAT: 16G; SODIUM: 114MG; CARBOHYDRATES: 58G; FIBER: 2G; PROTEIN: 6G

Blueberry clafouti

PREP: 5 MINUTES • PRESSURE: 11 MINUTES • TOTAL: 16 MINUTES • PRESSURE LEVEL: HIGH • RELEASE: QUICK
SERVES: 2

Ingredients

1 teaspoon unsalted butter, at room temperature, divided

½ cup fresh blueberries, divided

⅓ cup whole milk

3 tablespoons heavy (whipping) cream

3 tablespoons sugar

¼ cup all-purpose flour

1 large egg

¼ teaspoon vanilla extract

¼ teaspoon lemon zest

⅛ teaspoon ground cinnamon

Pinch fine salt

1 cup water, for steaming

2 teaspoons confectioners' sugar or powdered sugar

Directions:

1. **Preparing the ingredients**. Using ½ teaspoon of butter each, coat the insides of each of 2 custard cups or small ramekins. Put ¼ cup of blueberries in each cup.
   In a medium bowl, combine the milk, heavy cream, sugar, flour, egg, vanilla, lemon zest, cinnamon, and fine salt. Using a hand mixer, beat the ingredients for about 2 minutes on medium speed, or until the batter is smooth. Evenly divide the batter between the 2 cups, filling them about three-fourths full with batter.
   Add the water and insert the steamer basket or trivet. Place the custard cups on the steamer insert. Place a square of aluminum foil over the pan, but don't crimp it down; it's just to keep steam from condensing on the surface of the clafouti.
2. **High pressure for 11 minutes**. Lock the lid on the Ninja Foodi Multicooker® and then cook for 11 minutes. To get 11-minutes cook time, press "Pressure" button, and use the time adjustment button to adjust the cook time to 11 minutes.
3. **Pressure release.** Use the quick-release method.
4. **Air Frying and Finish the dish**. Unlock and remove the lid. Using tongs, remove the foil. Transfer the cups to a small baking sheet. Close the Crisping Lid, select BROIL, and set the time to 4 minutes. Select START/STOP to begin until the tops brown slightly. Cool for at least 10 minutes. Sift the confectioners' sugar over the clafouti, and serve warm.

Per serving: calories: 314; fat: 15g; sodium: 153mg; carbohydrates: 41g; fiber: 1g; protein: 7g

Apple Crumb Cake

PREP: 5 MINUTES • PRESSURE: 23 MINUTES • TOTAL: 30 MINUTES • PRESSURE LEVEL: HIGH • RELEASE: QUICK
SERVES: 2

Ingredients
2 small red apples
¾ cup melted butter
½ cup sugar
1½ cups water
⅔ cup dry bread crumbs
Juice and zest from ½ lemon
2 tbsp flour
1 tsp cinnamon
1 tsp ginger

Directions:
1. **Preparing the ingredients.** To make the filling, mix bread crumbs, sugar, cinnamon, melted butter, ginger, lemon juice, and lemon zest.
   Core the apples, leaving the peels on, and slice very thin.
   Grease your baking dish with butter and coat with a dusting flour. Lay down the apple slices in fan shapes.
   Add a layer of the crumb filling, followed by apples, and keep going until everything is used up.
   Wrap the dish tightly in foil. Pour 1½ cups of water into your Ninja Foodi Multicooker™ and lower in the trivet.
   Put the wrapped dish on top and seal the lid.
2. **High pressure for 23 minutes.** Select "Pressure" and cook at HIGH pressure for 23 minutes.
3. **Pressure release.** Once cooking is complete, press CANCEL and wait 10 minutes before quick-releasing.
4. **Air Frying and Finish the dish.** Take out the cake and remove the foil.
   To finish, sprinkle raw sugar on top, close the Crisping Lid, select BROIL, and set the time to 3 minutes. Select START/STOP to begin and broil for just 3 minutes, or until the sugar caramelizes. Serve!

Strawberry Shortcake Mug Cake

PREP: 5 MINUTES • PRESSURE: 12 MINUTES • TOTAL: 17 MINUTES • PRESSURE LEVEL: HIGH • RELEASE: QUICK

Ingredients
   1 egg
   ½ cup (48 g) almond flour
   ½ tsp 100% vanilla extract
   1 tbsp. (15 ml) maple syrup
   1 tbsp. (15 ml) ghee
   3 tbsp. (24 g) chopped strawberries (plus more for garnish)
   1 cup (240 ml) water
   3 tbsp. (45 ml) coconut whipped cream to garnish

Directions
1. **Preparing the Ingredients.** Combine all of the ingredients, except for the water and whipped cream, into a heat-resistant ceramic coffee mug.
   Pour the cup of water into the stainless steel Ninja Foodi® Multicooker bowl and place the wire rack into the basin. Set your mug on top of the rack and secure the lid.
2. **High pressure for 12 minutes.** Lock the lid, cook on high pressure for 12 minutes. To get 12-minutes cook time, press "pressure" button and adjust the time.
3. **Pressure Release.** Now allow the cake to cook, quick-releasing the pressure valve when the cycle is complete.
4. **Finish the dish.** Remove the lid when safe to do so and carefully remove the hot mug. Top with coconut whipped cream and additional fresh strawberries if desired.

Vanilla-Ginger Custard

PREP: 10 MINUTES • PRESSURE: 6 MINUTES • TOTAL: 16 MINUTES • PRESSURE LEVEL: HIGH • RELEASE: NATURAL

Ingredients
⅓ cup whole milk
⅓ cup heavy (whipping) cream
½ teaspoon vanilla extract
¼ teaspoon ground ginger
2 large egg yolks
⅓ cup granulated sugar
1 cup water, for steaming (double-check the Ninja Foodi® Multicooker manual to confirm amount, and follow the manual if there is a discrepancy)
2 teaspoons chopped crystalized ginger (optional)

Directions
1. **Preparing the Ingredients.** In a small saucepan set over medium heat, combine the milk, heavy cream, vanilla, and ground ginger, and bring the mixture just to a simmer. Take it off the heat and cool slightly.
   In a small bowl, whisk together the egg yolks and sugar until the sugar is dissolved and the mixture is pale yellow. Working slowly, whisk a few tablespoons of the milk mixture into the egg mixture, then repeat with a little more. Once the egg mixture is warmed, whisk in the remainder of the milk mixture.
   Pour the custard into 2 heatproof custard cups or small ramekins. Cover with aluminum foil, and crimp to seal around the edges.
   Add the water and insert the steamer basket or trivet.
   Place the custard cups on the steamer insert.
2. **High pressure for 6 minutes** Lock the lid in place, and bring the pot to high pressure. Cook at high pressure for 6 minutes. To get 6-minutes cook time, press "pressure" button and use the TIME ADJUSTMENT button to adjust the cook time to 6 minutes
3. **Pressure Release.** Use the natural method to release pressure.
4. **Finish the dish**. Unlock and remove the lid. Using tongs, carefully remove the custards from the cooker and remove the foil. The custards should be set but still a bit soft in the middle; they'll firm as they cool. Cool for 20 to 30 minutes, then refrigerate for several hours to chill completely. When ready to serve, top with the crystalized ginger.
5. Enjoy!

Poached Peach Cups with Ricotta and Honey

PREP: 5 MINUTES • PRESSURE: 4 MINUTES • TOTAL: 9 MINUTES • PRESSURE LEVEL: LOW • RELEASE: QUICK

Ingredients

4 peaches, cut in half and pitted
1/4 cup apple juice
1/4 cup water
3 tablespoons light brown sugar
1/8 teaspoon ground cinnamon
1 cup part-skim ricotta cheese
2 tablespoons honey
1/4 teaspoon vanilla extract

Directions

1. **Preparing the Ingredients.** Add peaches, apple juice, water, brown sugar, and cinnamon to the cooker.
2. **High pressure for 4 minutes.** Lock the lid on the Ninja Foodi® Multicooker and then cook for 4 minutes. To get 4-minutes cook time, press "pressure" button, and use the TIME ADJUSTMENT button to adjust the cook time to 4 minutes.
3. **Pressure Release.** Perform a quick release to release the cooker's pressure.
4. Remove peaches from cooking liquid, and set aside.
5. **Finish the dish.** Combine ricotta cheese, honey, and vanilla extract, and serve spooned into the center of each peach half.

Three-Ingredient Honey Flans

PREP: 5 MINUTES • PRESSURE: 5 MINUTES • TOTAL: 10 MINUTES • PRESSURE LEVEL: HIGH • RELEASE: NATURAL

Ingredients

2 large eggs

⅓ cup dark honey

1cup whole milk

8 amaretti cookies or gingersnaps, finely crushed, for sprinkling

Directions

1. **Preparing the Ingredients.** Add 2 cups of water to the Ninja Foodi® Multicooker base; insert the steamer basket and set aside.

   Break one of the eggs into a 4-cup measuring cup; separate the other egg, adding the yolk to the measuring cup and reserving the white for another use.

   Add the honey to the eggs and whisk together until well combined, then whisk in the milk. Pour the mixture through a fine-mesh strainer into six 4-ounce ramekins; cover each tightly with aluminum foil.

   Arrange the ramekins in the steamer basket, making sure they are level.

2. **High pressure for 5 minutes.** Close and lock the lid of the Ninja Foodi® Multicooker. Cook at high pressure for 5 minutes. To get 5-minutes cook time, press "pressure" button, and use the TIME ADJUSTMENT button to adjust the cook time to 5 minutes.

3. **Pressure Release.** When the time is up, open the Ninja Foodi® Multicooker using the 10-Minute Natural Release method.

4. **Finish the dish.** Check the flan for doneness. Lift the ramekins out of the cooker.

   Remove the foil and sprinkle crushed cookies over each flan and serve warm. Or if you prefer to serve them chilled, hold off on the crushed cookies. Instead, let the flans cool for about 30 minutes, then cover with plastic wrap and refrigerate.

   Add the crushed cookies just before serving.

Molten Gingerbread Cake

PREP: 5 MINUTES • PRESSURE: 15 MINUTES • TOTAL: 20 MINUTES • PRESSURE LEVEL: HIGH • RELEASE: COMBINATION

Ingredients

3 tablespoons very hot water
¼ cup vegetable oil
¼ cup packed brown sugar
¼ cup molasses
1 large egg
⅔ cup all-purpose flour
¾ teaspoon ground ginger
½ teaspoon ground cinnamon
¼ teaspoon kosher salt
¼ teaspoon baking powder
¼ teaspoon baking soda
1 cup water, for steaming (double-check the Ninja Foodi® Multicooker manual to confirm amount, and follow the manual if there is a discrepancy)

Directions

1. **Preparing the Ingredients.** In a small bowl, using a hand mixer, mix together the hot water, vegetable oil, brown sugar, molasses, and egg. In another small bowl, sift together the flour, ground ginger, cinnamon, kosher salt, baking powder, and baking soda. Add the dry ingredients to the liquid mixture. Mix on medium speed until the ingredients are thoroughly combined, with no lumps. Pour the batter into a nonstick mini (3-by-5-inch) loaf pan. Cover the pan with aluminum foil, making a dome over the pan.
   Add the water and insert the steamer basket or trivet. Carefully place the loaf pan on the steamer insert.
2. **High pressure for 15 minutes**. Lock the lid on the Ninja Foodi® Multicooker and then cook for 15 minutes. To get 15-minutes cook time, press "pressure"button and adjust the time.
   When the timer goes off, turn the cooker off. ("Warm" setting, turn off).
3. **Pressure Release.** After cooking, use the natural method to release pressure for 5 minutes, then the quick method to release the remaining pressure.
4. **Finish the dish.** Unlock and remove the lid. Using tongs, carefully remove the pan from the Ninja Foodi® Multicooker. Let the cake rest for 2 to 3 minutes; remove the foil, slice, and serve.

To sift the dry ingredients, place a medium-coarse sieve over a small bowl or on a sheet of wax paper or parchment paper. Measure the dry ingredients into the sieve. Tap the side of the sieve to move the contents through the sieve to the bowl or parchment paper; then transfer the sifted ingredients to the wet ingredients.

Vanilla Pots de Crème

PREP: 5 MINUTES • PRESSURE: 5 MINUTES • TOTAL: 10 MINUTES • PRESSURE LEVEL: HIGH • RELEASE: NATURAL

SERVES 2-4

Ingredients

6 large egg yolks
⅔ cup sugar
1 cup whole milk
1 cup heavy cream
1 teaspoon vanilla extract
Seasonal fruit, for serving

Directions

1. **Preparing the Ingredients.** Add 2 cups of water to the Ninja Foodi® Multicooker base; insert the steamer basket and set aside. In a large bowl, whisk together the egg yolks and sugar until the sugar has dissolved. Add the milk, cream, and vanilla, whisking just enough to combine; do not whip. Pour the mixture through a fine-mesh strainer into six 4-ounce ramekins; cover each tightly with aluminum foil. Arrange in the steamer basket, making sure they are level.

2. **High pressure for 5 minutes.** Close and lock the lid of the Ninja Foodi® Multicooker. Cook at high pressure for 5 minutes. To get 5-minutes cook time, press "pressure" button, and use the TIME ADJUSTMENT button to adjust the cook time to 5 minutes

3. **Pressure Release.** When the time is up, open the Ninja Foodi® Multicooker using the 10-Minute Natural Release method.

4. **Finish the dish.** Check the custard for doneness. Lift all the ramekins out of the cooker; remove the foil. Serve the pots de crème warm, topped with seasonal fruit. Or if you prefer to serve them chilled, let them cool for 30 to 45 minutes, then cover tightly with plastic wrap and refrigerate until chilled.
Add the fruit when serving.

Blueberry Clafouti

PREP: 5 MINUTES • PRESSURE: 11 MINUTES • TOTAL: 16 MINUTES • PRESSURE LEVEL: HIGH • RELEASE: QUICK
SERVES 2

Ingredients

1 teaspoon unsalted butter, at room temperature, divided
½ cup fresh blueberries, divided
⅓ cup whole milk
3 tablespoons heavy (whipping) cream
3 tablespoons sugar
¼ cup all-purpose flour
1 large egg
¼ teaspoon vanilla extract
¼ teaspoon lemon zest
⅛ teaspoon ground cinnamon
Pinch fine salt
1 cup water, for steaming (double-check the Ninja Foodi® Multicooker manual to confirm amount, and follow the manual if there is a discrepancy)
2 teaspoons confectioners' sugar or powdered sugar

Directions

1. **Preparing the Ingredients.** Using ½ teaspoon of butter each, coat the insides of each of 2 custard cups or small ramekins. Put ¼ cup of blueberries in each cup.

   In a medium bowl, combine the milk, heavy cream, sugar, flour, egg, vanilla, lemon zest, cinnamon, and fine salt. Using a hand mixer, beat the ingredients for about 2 minutes on medium speed, or until the batter is smooth. Evenly divide the batter between the 2 cups, filling them about three-fourths full with batter.

   Add the water and insert the steamer basket or trivet. Place the custard cups on the steamer insert. Place a square of aluminum foil over the pan, but don't crimp it down; it's just to keep steam from condensing on the surface of the clafouti.

2. **High pressure for 11 minutes.** Lock the lid on the Ninja Foodi® Multicooker and then cook for 11 minutes. To get 11-minutes cook time, press "pressure" button, and use the TIME ADJUSTMENT button to adjust the cook time to 11 minutes.

3. **Pressure release.** Use the quick-release method.

4. **Finish the dish.** Unlock and remove the lid. Using tongs, remove the foil. Transfer the cups to a small baking sheet. Preheat the broiler, and position a rack close to the broiler element. Place the baking sheet under the broiler for 3 to 4 minutes, or until the tops

brown slightly. Cool for at least 10 minutes. Sift the confectioners' sugar over the clafouti, and serve warm.

PER SERVING: CALORIES: 314; FAT: 15G; SODIUM: 153MG; CARBOHYDRATES: 41G; FIBER: 1G; PROTEIN: 7G

Strawberry Freezer Jam Recipe

PREP: 10 MINUTES • PRESSURE: 8 MINUTES • TOTAL: 18 MINUTES • PRESSURE LEVEL: HIGH • RELEASE: NATURAL
SERVES 4 CUPS

Ingredients

    1 lb. (450 grams) strawberries (fresh or frozen)
    1 /2 to 1 lb. (225 to 450 grams) granulated sugar
    1 navel orange
    1 tbs. butter (optional, vegans can omit)

Directions

1. **Preparing the Ingredients.** If you are using fresh berries, remove the stems, leaves and any bruised spots from the strawberries, lightly wash them, and cut into halves or quarters, depending on size. For frozen berries, defrost before use, cut them up if necessary.

   Peel the navel orange, removing the bitter white pith and any white connective tissues. I do this by slicing a bit off the top, so I can see how thick the peel is. I then take the knife and cut slices of peel down the sides of the orange. (It is better to remove a little of the orange than to leave the bitter pith on the orange.) Once you have removed all the peel and any pith attached to the outside of the orange, break it apart into segments, remove any white pithy connective tissues inside, and roughly chop the segments. Reserve the chopped segments and any juice.

   For a very smooth jam, place the sliced strawberries and chopped orange segments and juice into a food processor or blender and puree until smooth, then add to the sugar. If you would like your jam more like preserves (with small pieces of fruit mixed in), combine the sliced strawberries, orange pieces, and orange juice into the sugar.

   Once mixed, use a potato masher to roughly mash the strawberries. The mixture should macerate in the refrigerator for at least an hour, but if you can let it set for 8 – 24 hours, that's even better.

   Once the mixture has macerated, add to the Ninja Foodi® Multicooker. Using the "Sauté" setting, bring the jam up to a hard boil for 3 minutes to dissolve the sugar and reduce the excess water content. Stir frequently with the longest handled spatula you own.

   Stir in 1 tablespoon of butter

2. **High pressure for 8 minutes.** Lock the lid on the Ninja Foodi® Multicooker and then cook for 8 minutes. To get 8-minutes cook time, press "pressure" button, and use the TIME ADJUSTMENT button to adjust the cook time to 8 minutes.

3. **Pressure Release.** Let its pressure return to normal naturally, 8 to 12 minutes.

4. **Finish the dish.** After pressure has released, unlock and remove the lid, tilting the front side down and the back side up to direct any residual heat and steam away from you. With the lid OFF and the "Sauté" setting, bring the mixture back to the boil for 3 minutes, stirring frequently. Turn the unit off after the 3 minutes are up. Allow mixture to cool to room temperature, stirring periodically. Once cooled, put the jam in a container in the refrigerator to finish setting.

HERITAGE OF FOOD: A FAMILY GATHERING

To survive, we need to eat. As a result, food has turned into a symbol of loving, nurturing and sharing with one another. Recording, collecting, sharing and remembering the recipes that have been passed to you by your family is a great way to immortalize and honor your family. It is these traditions that carve out your individual personality. You will not just be honoring your family tradition by cooking these recipes but they will also inspire you to create your own variations, which you can then pass on to your children's.

The recipes are just passed on by everyone and nobody actually possesses them. I too love sharing recipes. The collection is vibrant and rich as a number of home cooks have offered their inputs to ensure that all of us can cook delicious meals at our home. I am thankful to each one of you who has contributed to this book and has allowed their traditions to pass on and grow with others. You guys are really wonderful!

I am also thankful to the cooks who have evaluated all these recipes. You're, as well as, the comments that came from your family members and friends were really invaluable.

If you have the time and inclination, please consider leaving a short review wherever you can, we would love to learn more about your opinion.

https://www.amazon.com/review/review-your-purchases/

About the Author

Barbara is a Washington-based experienced chef. She is known for her culinary skills and her high standards. She commits to making possible for everyone to cook, even if they have too little time. She enjoys combining the classic recipes with the modern cooking technology like Electric Pressure Cooker, and home sous vide immersion circulator machine. The best results of his experiments she shares with the others - by writing books.

28089992R00087